It's Quicker
By Rail!

It's Quicker By Rail!

THE HISTORY OF LNER ADVERTISING

Allan Middleton

TEMPUS

First published 2002

PUBLISHED IN THE UNITED KINGDOM BY:
Tempus Publishing Ltd
The Mill, Brimscombe Port
Stroud, Gloucestershire GL5 2QG

PUBLISHED IN THE UNITED STATES OF AMERICA BY:
Tempus Publishing Inc.
2 Cumberland Street
Charleston, SC 29401

British Library Cataloguing in Publication Data.
A catalogue record for this book is available from the British Library.

ISBN 0 7524 2765 2

Typesetting and origination by Tempus Publishing.
Printed in Great Britain by Midway Colour Print, Wiltshire

CONTENTS

ACKNOWLEDGEMENTS

I have received a great deal of help in producing this work and must thank the staff of the Public Records Office at Kew and the staff of the British Library. Patrick Bogue of Onslows Auctioneers and John Jenkins formerly of the same company. My thanks also to Malcolm Guest and Ian Wright.

   I must not forget my two very good and sadly now departed friends Bob Cole and John Holt for their enthusiasm and encouragement over many years. Last but not least I must thank my son Anthony for the loan of much of his collection.

INTRODUCTION

My enthusiasm for railways was born in 1939 when, at a very early age and because of the Second World War, I was evacuated by train with my south London school to Paignton in Devon. My stay there was for only a few months and, because of being very homesick and the fact that the expected bombing of London did not materialise, I came back home.

Subsequently the Blitz on London saw me being evacuated once again, this time with my parents, to relations in Newbury, Berkshire. I well remember my mother buying me one of the very first Ian Allan ABCs of Great Western Locomotives and the many happy hours spent on the platform at Newbury watching such trains as the Cornish Riviera and the Torbay Express go roaring through.

From time to time I returned to London by the Great Western and the Southern Railways respectively. My earliest recollection of railway publicity was seeing the rows of coloured handbills hanging on loops of string from a row of nails. These I collected avidly and now wished I had taken greater care of.

Leaving school and starting work, my interest in railways slumbered for some years, until in the late 1960s when I suddenly found that much of what I knew of railways was fast disappearing. My particular interest in railway publicity was reawakened in the early 1970s with the purchase of a copy of the late Roger Burdett Wilson's excellent book *'Go Great Western' A History of GWR Publicity*.

My somewhat enforced early retirement in the 1980s allowed me the time to study my interest in more detail and the LNER's publicity in particular. There comes a time in all research when new information is very slow in coming and what to do with the information already to hand?

The result of my studies is this book, which I hope may at least form some sort of base to which others may add. I am sure that errors will be found in my work and I must accept full blame where these may occur but I hope these will not distract from the overall pleasure of looking back at the publicity of that great railway company The London & North Eastern.

Allan Middleton
Caterham, Surrey

Chapter One

THE ADVERTISING
DEPARTMENT

'Its Quicker By Rail', we were told by the LNER advertisements of the 1930s. We were also informed that it should be 'Scotland for the Holidays' and 'Harwich for the Continent'. They would try to convince us that we should 'Meet the Sun on the East Coast', which was of course 'On the Drier Side'. It was 'Marylebone for the Midlands', and it was said at the time that when buses stopped outside the LNER's main London terminus, the conductors would call out 'Kings Cross for Scotland'.

POWER · GRACE · SPEED

KING'S CROSS

FOR

SCOTLAND

EAST COAST ROUTE
SHORTEST & QUICKEST

EASE & COMFORT

LONDON &
NORTH EASTERN

Press advertising was by far the largest item on the LNER's advertising budget. This advertisement from the national press of March 1929.

SCOTLAND

FOR HOLIDAYS

EAST COAST ROUTE

SHORTEST AND QUICKEST

DIRECTLY SERVES
EDINBURGH AND THE LOWLANDS,
ABERDEEN & THE DEE, DON & SPEY VALLEYS,
INVERNESS & THE NORTHERN HIGHLANDS,
GLASGOW, THE CLYDE RESORTS, AND
THE WESTERN HIGHLANDS AND ISLANDS.

THROUGH RESTAURANT AND SLEEPING CAR EXPRESSES

OBTAIN ILLUSTRATED BOOKLETS AND HOTELS AND
LODGINGS GUIDE FROM ANY L N E R OFFICE, OR THE
PASSENGER MANAGERS AT LIVERPOOL STREET STATION,
LONDON, E C 2, YORK, WAVERLEY STATION, EDIN
BURGH, OR THE TRAFFIC SUPERINTENDENT, L N E R,
ABERDEEN

TRAVEL BY
EAST COAST ROUTE

Some of the early press advertisements were not very inspiring. This example is from *Country Life* magazine of May 1923.

This advertisement appeared in most of the national newspapers early in 1923. It gave the constituent companies of the LNER and the new company's name and aims.

At the same time that these slogans were being proclaimed, the LNER's famous trains were making the headlines. *The Flying Scotsman*, the *Queen of Scots* and later the *Silver Jubilee* and the *Coronation*, were all 'grist to the Advertising Department's mill'.

There must surely be a reason why, some sixty years after these trains were making the news, such magical names still come to mind. Without doubt much of the reason why we still remember these trains must come from the publicity and ballyhoo that was generated at the time, and seems by one means or another to have been passed down through the years.

It is a fact that the lifetime of the LNER was only of some twenty-five years duration, but during that time the company led the way in many aspects of railway operation. It could certainly be said to have been a railway company of innovation.

The LNER had always tried to live up to its motto 'Forward' and the second half of the 1930s had seen the company building a new image when its streamlined trains were breaking records for speed and comfort. Its advertising policy was never brash or forceful, and always tried to convey a feeling of propriety and quality.

It was on 1 January 1923 that the London & North Eastern Railway Co. was formed by the amalgamation of six very diverse railway companies, as well as several smaller subsidiary companies. There were also two major joint lines, both of which were run jointly with the London Midland & Scottish Railway.

The first public announcement, and therefore the first item of publicity from the new company, was placed in most of the national newspapers and appeared as posters on all stations. It was a straightforward statement that said 'Our New Name. London and North Eastern Railway. Our Aim, To Serve You!

Coinciding with this announcement, the company published a small booklet entitled 'At Your Service'. Strangely this booklet was actually headed 'Eastern Group of Railways', so presumably the new company's name had not been announced at the time of printing.

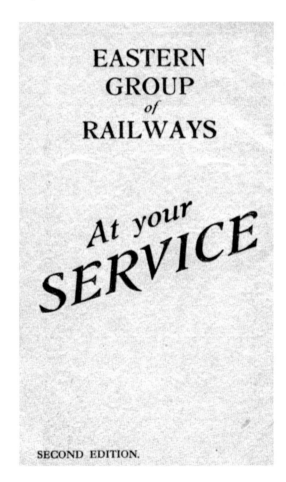

This booklet pre-dated the press advertisements for the 1923 grouping. It can be seen that it referred to the Eastern Group of Railways, as at that time the name London & North Eastern had not been agreed. The booklet detailed the new company's area of operation and the various services that were to be offered.

L·N·E·R
OPENING OF NEW LINE
CUFFLEY
TO STEVENAGE

On MONDAY, 2nd JUNE, 1924, the Loop Line Extension from Cuffley to Stevenage will be opened for Passenger Traffic, also for General Merchandise—not requiring Warehousing or Cartage by Railway Teams—and Coal. The Stations on the New Line will be as under :—

BAYFORD
HERTFORD NORTH
STAPLEFORD
WATTON

The Company's present Hertford North Station (on the Hatfield and Hertford Branch) will be closed for Passenger and Parcels Traffic after Sunday, 1st June, 1924. General Merchandise and Coal Traffic will continue to be dealt with at that Station as hitherto.

Parcels traffic will be dealt with at Bayford and Hertford North.

Passenger trains on the Hatfield and Hertford Branch will run to and from Hertford North Station on the New Line on and from Monday, 2nd June.

Important alterations will be made in the Suburban and City Train Services and the Hatfield and Hertford Branch Service on and after Monday, 2nd June, and passengers are requested to consult the Company's Sheet Time Tables and Notices.

Full particulars as to Fares and Season Ticket Rates may be obtained from the Passenger Manager, Liverpool Street Station, London, E.C. 2.

LONDON, May, 1924.

Waterlow & Sons Limited, London, Dunstable & Watford.

An early example of the LNER's handbills. This one printed in May 1924 has a very presentable appearance and gives details of the new line to be opened between Cuffley and Stevenage. This form of the company's initials should be noted.

L·N·E·R
ADDITIONAL
TRAM ARRANGEMENTS
Wisbech & Upwell

WEEKDAYS

On and from Monday, 25th August the 4.25 p.m. (Saturdays only) Wisbech to Upwell, & 5.15 p.m. (Saturdays only) Upwell to Wisbech will run each weekday.

London, August, 1924.

Another well presented early handbill. This example was printed in the company's own works in August 1924. Again the LNER initials should be noted, this time enclosed.

It had been the job of Ralph Wedgwood and the Organisation Committee to set up the management and organisation of the new company. The aim was to avoid too much centralisation in London and, with this in mind, the system was divided into three areas, namely; Southern, which incorporated the former Great Northern, Great Eastern and Great Central Railway's, with headquarters at Liverpool Street; North Eastern, with headquarters at York; and Scottish Area, which was the former North British and Great North of Scotland Railways, with headquarters at Edinburgh.

Each area had an Area General Manager who was directly responsible to the Chief General Manager, whose office was at the new company's headquarters at Kings Cross. Other managerial appointments were made by Ralph Wedgwood, one of which was W.M. Teasdale, who was given the position of Advertising Manager.

W.M. Teasdale came from the North Eastern Railway, where among other appointments he had been Trade Advertising Agent. As the North Eastern's Trade Advertising Agent, he had also been responsible for traffic advertising, so he was not without the necessary experience. Teasdale was to hold the new position for some four years until late 1927, when he was promoted to Assistant General Manager.

Circular No.11 from the Chief General Manager, Ralph Wedgewood, sets out the terms of appointment for the LNER's first Advertising Manager.

LONDON AND NORTH EASTERN RAILWAY

CHIEF GENERAL MANAGER'S OFFICE,
KING'S CROSS,

Circular No. 11

14th April, 1923.

MR. W. M. TEASDALE has been appointed Advertising Manager for the whole line. His temporary address is 1, The Abbey Garden, Westminster, S.W.1. but he will remove shortly to offices at King's Cross.

The Advertising Manager will be responsible for :—

The compilation and issue of all advertisements.
All advertising expenditure.
The appearance of the Company's property so far as advertisements are concerned.
The use of space suitable for advertising purposes upon the Company's property which is not required for the working of the Railway, in consultation with any other Department concerned.
All trade advertisements.

In order to avoid delay the Advertising Manager will have offices at Edinburgh, York and London (26, Pancras Road, N.W. 1.). Matters local to each Area will be dealt with through these Offices, and the Advertising Manager will be directly responsible for this work to each Area General Manager. The Departmental Officers in each Area should keep the Advertising Manager's Area Office posted with the necessary data for the compilation of advertisements, but on urgent or detail matters the Advertising Manager will be at liberty to communicate direct with the District Officers and Station Masters.

R. L. WEDGWOOD.

13

In May 1924 a circular was issued by the Chief General Manager, referring to the setting up of a Press Section within the Advertising Department. It was to be the Press Section's responsibility to keep the public informed, via the national press, of the company's activities and points of view, especially on such controversial subjects as railway charges, standards of service and increasing competition from the roads.

This arrangement of having the Press Section as part of the Advertising Department was more or less standard practice. However, early in 1928 the LNER took the unusual step of removing the Section from the control of the Advertising Manager, and attached it directly to the Chief General Manager's office under the charge of an Information Agent.

Although it was said that close collaboration would still be necessary between the Advertising Department and the Information Agent, the implication was that contact with the press would be better coming from a department where more up-to-date information was available on the day-to-day running of the railway.

There was, however, a much more subtle reason for the change and that was the fact that the Advertising Department spent a lot of money in advertising in certain newspapers. It was felt that in order to avoid any bias, the department issuing press notices should be separated from the department involved in buying advertising space. This was to try to ensure that the LNER was given as much news coverage in those newspapers they did not advertise in, as those they patronised.

It is well known that W.M. Teasdale was one of the first Advertising Managers to commission artists of some repute, and these were particularly put to work on the company's pictorial posters. This approach won Teasdale a great deal of respect in the advertising world. It has been mentioned that Teasdale was promoted to Assistant Chief General Manager in 1927, a position he held for five years when, to much surprise, he resigned to become a Director of Allied Newspapers. He died in 1948 at the age of fifty-nine.

The man appointed to succeed Teasdale as Advertising Manager was C.G.G. Dandridge, who took up the post at Kings Cross on 1 January 1928. He was only to reside at Kings Cross for eighteen months, for in June 1929 the Advertising Manager's office was moved to Marylebone.

Dandridge started his railway career in 1905 in the General Manager's office of the Great Central Railway where he passed the required exams to enter the Great Central's training scheme. During the First World War he was with the traffic office of the British Army in France, rising to the rank of Major. In 1918 he took charge of the Traffic Department of the Archangel Northern Railway in Russia. It was while he was in Russia that he met Princess Olga Galitzin, whom he was later to marry in England.

On his return to England, Dandridge was made Assistant District Traffic Manager at Manchester, followed shortly after by promotion to District Passenger Manager in London. Following Teasdale's promotion, Dandridge was offered the position of Advertising Manager, which he was to retain almost to Nationalisation.

A few months after taking up his new post, Dandridge forwarded an article on advertising to the editor of the *LNER Magazine*. This appeared in the magazine for December 1928, and was entitled 'Advertising Notes'. He wrote a foreword to his article in which he said: 'The great interest taken in advertising, and the number of suggestions received each month by the Advertising Department, are I think sufficient justification for the inclusion of a few notes on this subject in each issue of our home journal'.

He went on to say 'There is much evidence of individual thought about propaganda at the present time, and constructive ideas will always be encouraged. The Advertising Department on the other hand is anxious that its policy and activities should be followed and understood, and I am conscious of the value of co-operation if we are to make the best use of our resources'.

Dandridge was to continue his Advertising Notes feature in the magazine up to the middle of the Second World War, when they ceased through lack of space owing to wartime conditions. Although Dandridge's Advertising Notes were always of a fairly brief nature, they can be of help to anyone researching the LNER's advertising activities between 1929 and 1942.

Like Teasdale before him, Dandridge represented the LNER on the Railway Clearing House Advertising Representatives Committee, and was chairman for the year on at least two occasions. This committee had been set up in an end-eavour to make sure that the four main line companies individual advertising policies were in some sort of accordance with each other and to present a united opinion in respect of other competition.

It is probably not generally known quite how much the four companies liaised with each other so far as their advertising was concerned. There were certainly differences of opinion between them, perhaps particularly between Dandridge and Cuthbert Graseman, who was Dandridge's counterpart on the Southern, but as the years progressed into the mid and late 1930s, the four companies spoke more and more with one voice.

It was as early as July 1928, when, at a meeting of the RCH Advertising Representatives, the idea of joint press advertisements for the following year's Bank Holidays was put forward. The idea had the full approval of all four General Managers, and the first combined newspaper advertisements were run during November 1928.

The first ever advertisement published jointly by the four main line companies in the national press, was placed by the LMS in December 1929. It was the turn of the LNER to provide the advertisement for the following Easter, and this design by Montague Black appeared in most national newspapers at that time.

One task that was taken on by the Railway Clearing House Advertising Committee, was the more or less annual publishing of a small booklet entitled *Facts About British Railways*. This booklet gave general railway statistics that was thought to be good publicity.

When it came to the question of getting the booklet printed for 1932, Dandridge put forward the suggestion that the LNER Printing Works should tender for the actual printing contract.

It was the normal practice of the committee to share out the work of designing any joint advertisements, etc., which were then put out to various printers for quotation. When Dandridge put forward his suggestion that the LNER should tender, there appeared to be a feeling that he was trying to be one up on the other companies. There seemed to be considerable embarrassment at his offer and, quoting from the minutes of the committee meeting:

With regard to the question of inviting the railway companies printing departments to tender for the printing of the booklet, it was agreed to report that the railway companies (except the London & North Eastern Co.) have no printing machinery capable of undertaking work of the magnitude of printing 20,000 booklets of the character of the 'Facts About British Railways' book. The following competitive tenders were therefore submitted:

	£	s	d
Wellington Printers Ltd	127	10	0
Knapp Drewett & Son	129	10	0
LNER Printing Works	130	0	0
Waterlow & Sons	137	0	0
Bemrose & Sons Ltd	145	0	0

One could almost hear the other companies representatives' sigh of relief when it was pointed out that the LNER's Printing Works had not submitted the lowest tender and it was decided to accept the tender of Wellington Printers Ltd.

Perhaps a word here about the LNER's Printing Works. The building itself was quite a large structure, being some 350ft long, with four floors. It was erected by the Great Eastern Railway in 1892, adjacent to Stratford Market Station in East London.

The works was by far the largest printing facility belonging to any of the railway companies and in fact, in its heyday, over 250 staff were employed there. The works came under the control of the Stores Superintendent, and a considerable amount of the company's advertising material was produced there. They also printed the LNER Magazine, stationery, timetables, tickets, luggage labels and weekly notices among other items. The building, now well past one hundred years old, still stands, but is no longer in railway use.

Although a lot of the advertising material was printed at the company's works it was, relatively speaking, only a small proportion of the total. It was normal practice for each of the area advertising offices to put their letterpress work out to printers for quotation, and the successful firm would not only be given the contract to print the poster or handbill, but the layout and design would be left to them as well, certainly the typeface would be chosen by the printer from the particular styles that he had available.

All credit must be given to Cecil Dandridge, who for some time had been aware that something had to be done to improve the appearance of the company's printed material. He realised that the existing rather disorganised and old fashioned appearance had to be improved upon. It was obvious that what was really required was that all advertising material should be designed by one central office but, because

The LNER's own printing works at what was then known as Stratford Market, was by far the largest of any of the railway companies. This picture taken in recent times gives some idea of the size of the building.

of the huge amount of printed material that was produced, this would be impossible. He knew he could do nothing about the design and layout, but he had the idea that if all of the company's printed material used the same typeface this would considerably improve the overall appearance.

Dandridge had made the acquaintance of the well-known sculptor and designer Eric Gill and, during conversation with him in 1928, learnt that he was completing design work on a completely new typeface that had been commissioned by the Monotype Corporation, a large manufacturer of typecasting machinery. The new typeface was to be known as Gill Sans (referring to the omission of serifs) and it was in this new design that Dandridge saw an answer to his problem.

It was obvious to Dandridge that in order to present an entirely uniform picture throughout the company, the new lettering should not be confined to printed material but should extend to all of the company's signs, vehicles, etc.

It was going to be a lengthy task persuading all of the company's contract printers to carry the new Gill Sans type, but the company's business was highly valued and it was a case of move with the times or lose the company's work. It was not until 1932 that the company's own printing works were able to announce that they were fully equipped with the new type.

CHEAP EXCURSION BY L·N·E·R TO

Ashburys for Belle Vue

AND

MANCHESTER

MONDAY, 3rd SEPTEMBER, 1928.

On the above day, A SPECIAL TRAIN will leave	RETURN FARES, THIRD CLASS.	
a.m.	To Ashburys	To Manchester
MANSFIELD (LNE) 7-35	7/0	7/0
Warsop - - 7-50	6/0	6/0

Children under 12 years of age half-fare.

Reduced Admission to BELLE VUE: Adults 6d., Children 3d. on showing the Excursion Ticket.

Returning from MANCHESTER (London Road Station), same evening, at 11-20 p.m.; and from ASHBURYS STATION (within a few minutes' walk of the Gardens) at 11-25 p.m., after the Fireworks at Belle Vue. On the return journey Manchester passengers may join the train at Ashburys Station, after the Fireworks at Belle Vue.

Saloons for Parties £1.—Apply at once to local Station Master. Tickets, Bills, and all particulars may be obtained at the Stations; or from Messrs. King and Bird, Leeming Street, Mansfield

The CRESWELL COLLIERY BAND will take part in the Contest.

The 76th Annual
SEPTEMBER
CHAMPIONSHIP
BRASS BAND CONTEST

Commencing at 1-30 p.m.

The following Bands have been selected to compete :—

Amington, Tamworth	Glasbury
Barrow Shipyard	Harton Colliery, South Shields
Baxendale's (Manchester) Works	Hebden Bridge
Bentley Colliery, Doncaster	Irwell Springs, Bacup
Blackpool Excelsior	Milnrow Public
Callender's Cable Works	Nantlle Vale Royal, Wales
Carlton Main Frickley Colliery	Nelson Old
Creswell Colliery, Mansfield	Nutgrove, St. Helens
Dannemora Steel Works, Sheffield	Pendleton Public
Dove Holes Public	Rothwell Temperance
Eccles Borough	Royal Oakeley, Wales
Foden's Motor Works, Sandbach	Wingates Temperance

£2,000 GOLD TROPHY For Annual Competition

Cash Prizes, **£250** and other Prizes to value of over **£160** including *the* 50-GUINEA CHAMPION CHALLENGE CUP.

Each of the competing Bands will play the Tone Poem, "LORENZO," specially composed for this Contest by Dr. Thomas Keighley, Hon. Fellow, R.M.C.M. Conductors' Copies of Music, 1/-; by post, 1/1½. Programmes, 2d.; by post, 2½d.

NUMBERED RESERVED SEATS for the Contest, 2/4 and 3/6 each (including Tax), may be booked now.

In the evening will be presented a Magnificent Spectacular Display of

FIREWORKS

Extensive ZOOLOGICAL COLLECTION. Elephant Rides / Camel Rides

GREAT PLEASURE PARK	DANCING
New Children's Playground.	Max Erard's Famous Organ and Band
Scenic Railway. Miniature Railway.	NEW RESTAURANTS.

Great Football Match : Blackburn Rovers v. Manchester Central.

TICKETS AT THE STATIONS. Printed at the Zoological Gardens, Belle Vue, Manchester

This handbill is an example of collaborative advertising with a promoter. As can be seen it was for a cheap excursion to Ashburys Station which was a few minutes walk from Manchester's famous Belle Vue Gardens and Pleasure Park.

FROM YOUR WAREHOUSE TO YOUR CUSTOMER WITHOUT HANDLING BY MEANS OF

L·N·E·R CONTAINERS

Information at any L·N·E·R Goods Depôt or Office

LONDON & NORTH EASTERN RAILWAY

In 1928 it was felt that the LNER's goods services should be brought more to the attention of the general public, and this double royal poster was produced by Austin Cooper for that purpose. A picture of this poster appeared in the first Advertising Notes in the *LNER Magazine* in December 1928.

A serious-looking group at Kings Cross shows Eric Gill (first left with beret) and Cecil Dandridge (right foreground with bowler) together with other LNER management. The picture was taken on 21 November 1932 at a ceremony to mark the LNER's conversion to the use of Eric Gill's new Gill Sans typeface.

The Advertising Department, who was always on the lookout for some good publicity, thought they should have something of a launching ceremony to let it be known that the LNER had more or less completed the letter standardisation. In this they were aided by the Monotype Corporation, who no doubt had secured some good business from the venture. Dandridge asked Eric Gill to personally hand paint a new headboard (in Gill Sans of course) for the *Flying Scotsman*, and on 21 November 1932 a small ceremony was held at Kings Cross. It was said that part of Eric Gill's fee was to include a ride on the footplate of the locomotive.

In 1930 it was thought that it would be a good idea to let the public know how the company was performing from the financial point of view, and to this end the artist Austin Cooper was given the rather unusual commission to produce a quad royal poster showing the company's earnings and expenditure for the previous year. Cooper's sketch design, for which he was paid £10, showed two 'pie charts' giving the various financial results for 1929. The idea must have been considered successful, as it was repeated the following year. The 1930 'results' poster featured a rather colourful 'bar chart' design, but no doubt because of the worsening financial position, the 'results' posters do not seem to have been repeated in subsequent years.

Some of the earliest items of LNER advertising material were printed with a large 'totem' (perhaps better known today as a logo). This 'totem' carried the company name in full, but from about mid-1924 until the end of 1929 a smaller version of the same design was used with the LNER initials only. From 1929 until 1931 a diamond-shaped 'totem' enclosing the LNER initials was used on some publicity material, stations and road vehicles. It did not, however, appear to have any great artistic merit and did not seem to catch on.

It was during 1932 that, following the success of Eric Gill's new typeface, he was asked to design a new 'totem' for the company. Gill's original elliptical-shaped design had the LNER initials linked together, and this version was used up to 1934. Gill's new totem did have a somewhat ungainly appearance, and during 1934 it was altered so that each of the initials was separated. This alteration produced a much more balanced design, and this totem was used extensively up to nationalisation.

1930 saw the second year of the somewhat strange quad royal 'Results' posters, which gave a summary of the company's accounts for that year. Austin Cooper was paid £10 for the design.

For several years it had been realised that although the Advertising Department was striving to produce the best quality publicity material, their efforts were often wasted by poor presentation at the stations. In order to improve this situation, Dandridge published a hard-backed booklet that for obvious reasons became known as 'the green book'. Its official and rather longwinded title was *Selling LNER Transport By The Help of The Advertising Department*. The book gave strict instructions on the use and display of all types of posters, handbills, etc., and even gave information on how the paste for the posters was to be mixed. The original book was published in April 1929 and, through several amendments, was still being used well into nationalisation.

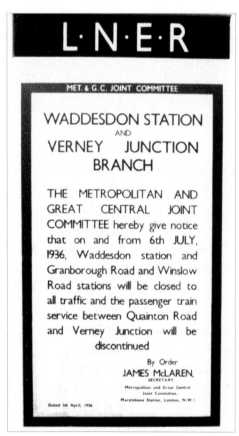

A typical example of the LNER's standard letterpress poster of the period. This double royal shows the closure of the Metropolitan & Great Central Waddesdon Station and Verney Junction Branch in 1936. Of necessity the poster is somewhat wordy, but is very easily read with its layout and Gill Sans typeface.

Frank Newbould's double royal was produced for the jointly run four main line companies 1936 scheme to sell rail freight facilities. Newbould did the artwork for the whole advertising package, which comprised posters, folders, press notices etc.

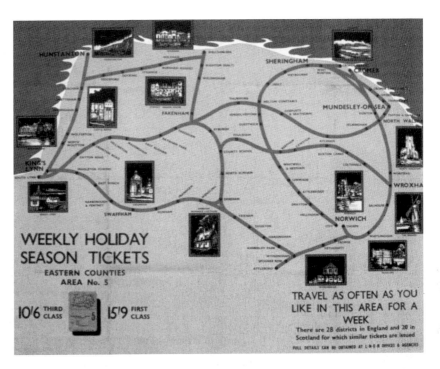

Weekly Holiday season tickets were just one of the LNER's many original ideas and, annually, posters, folders etc. were produced to advertise the facility. The quad royal shown is of 1937 vintage and shows the extent of area no.5.

By the mid–1930s, the four main line companies began to realise that some of their freight traffic was being lost to the increasing number of road hauliers. With this in mind a big joint advertising campaign was put in motion. For the LNER's part in this, an excellent sixteen-page booklet was produced with the title *Advertising of Freight Traffic Facilities, Notes For Goods Agents and Others*. In spite of another long-winded title, (a common fault of the time) this booklet was really well produced.

The idea behind the booklet was to give staff information about the joint publicity scheme and details of the advertising material that was to be made available. The booklet had illustrations of the posters, folders and press advertisements that were to be used, all of which were designed by Frank Newbould.

No doubt the success of the Advertising Freight booklet led the Advertising Department to produce a similar sixteen-page booklet entitled *Advertising of Passenger Train Facilities, Notes for Station Masters and Others*. Again this booklet which was to be circulated to staff, contained many illustrations of the current posters and folders dealing with Weekly Holiday Season Tickets, Rambling, Camping Coaches and the LNER's Save to Travel Scheme etc.

Generally speaking, the second half of the 1930s saw business increasing and this, together with the introduction of the streamline train services, kept the Advertising Department busy during this period.

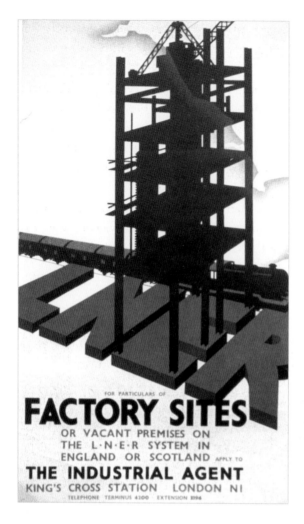

FOR PARTICULARS OF

FACTORY SITES
OR VACANT PREMISES ON
THE L·N·E·R SYSTEM IN
ENGLAND OR SCOTLAND APPLY TO
THE INDUSTRIAL AGENT
KING'S CROSS STATION   LONDON N1
TELEPHONE TERMINUS 4200   EXTENSION 1196

The reason behind the *Factory Sites* poster was to encourage the building of factories and warehouses adjoining the railway, so that direct rail connections could be laid which would ensure that the owners would use the LNER system. This poster again by Frank Newbould.

Late in 1938, and because of increasing competition from the roads, the four main line companies were planning a massive campaign to persuade the government to lift the legal restrictions on the way the railway companies were required to charge for the conveyance of freight traffic.

These laws, many of which had been laid down in the mid–1800s, were passed because of the complete monopoly the railways had in those times. During the 1930s, the railways were beginning to feel aggrieved that the road hauliers were able to charge as much or as little as they liked, whereas the railways were always obliged to charge in accordance with their massive list of fixed charges for every conceivable item.

This, the railways were saying, did not let them compete on fair terms with road transport. The Square Deal Campaign, which was the name put on the railways' big effort by Sir Ralph Wedgwood, the LNER's general manager, was launched in November 1938, with a great deal of press advertising backed up with numerous posters and handbills.

Unfortunately early spring was the busy time for the Advertising Department and The Square Deal campaign had to be left for the more pressing business of the forthcoming holiday season, which for 1939 was promising to be the busiest yet.

For the 1939 summer holiday campaign, Dandridge came up with the slogan 'Meet the Sun on the East Coast', which was to be the catchphrase used on all the holiday posters and handbills that summer.

The Meet the Sun campaign was progressing well, but had for some weeks been clouded over by the political situation in Europe. On 3 September war was declared and all thoughts of 'meeting the sun' came to an abrupt halt, at least for the time being.

A moment of relaxation for Cecil Dandridge (left) and his long-serving assistant, Francis Goodricke. The picture was taken in the grounds of 'The Chilterns' which was the temporary HQ of the Advertising Department during the Second World War.

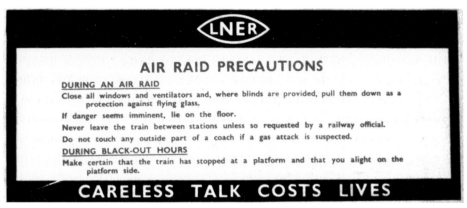

During the Second World War, standard air raid precaution carriage panels were provided for all four main line railway companies. This however is the LNER's up-market version.

Much of the history of the LNER during the Second World War has been fairly well documented, and probably nowhere better than in the company's own book *By Rail To Victory*. However, very little information has been recorded about the work of the Advertising Department during this period.

Shortly after the declaration of war, the Advertising Managers of each of the four main line companies, together with London Transport, were asked to form what was to be known as the British Railways Advertising Committee. The committee was formed to report to, and act upon the decisions of the Railway Executive.

It had already been arranged that upon the declaration of war, the Chief Officers and staff of the LNER would be evacuated from London to a large house known as the 'Hoo' and which was located near Welwyn in Hertfordshire. For security reasons the 'Hoo' was to be referred to by its code name HQ1.

There was not enough space at HQ1 for all departments, and the Advertising Department was initially moved partly to York and partly to the station waiting rooms at Stevenage, which was recorded as being 'most unsatisfactory'.

Early in 1940 the Department was able to lease a large house known as 'The Chilterns' which was at 48 London Road, Stevenage, and where the Department was all housed under one roof. It was, of course, not known at the time, but the Headquarters staff would not move back to London for five years.

During the first few days of war, instructions were issued to all stations to clean down all poster boards. Existing pictorial holiday posters, however, were to be left as some attempt to brighten up what was going to be a pretty gloomy situation.

It was by government order that the LNER had to remove or overpaint all station name signs. At some stations the staff had worked for years to provide the name in whitewashed stones, privet hedging and even flowerbed arrangements, but all had to go in order, it was said, that low flying enemy aircraft would not be able to navigate by reading the station name.

The Advertising Department was kept very busy producing a series of letterpress posters giving details of the new emergency services, directions to air raid shelters, etc. All carriage panels advertising cheap tickets and other such facilities had to be removed from carriages, and these were replaced with ARP (air raid precautions) announcements and watercolour carriage prints. All map posters and any publication containing maps were withdrawn, for there was a great fear at the time that enemy parachutists would be dropped. More than fifty years on, some of the regulations and restrictions seem almost laughable, but at the time it all seemed very relevant.

The sudden German invasion of much of Europe during April/May 1940 meant that the previously planned additional summer holiday trains were cancelled, to make way for extra troop trains. It was about this time that the Advertising Manager took an idea for a series of posters to the Railway Executive Committee. The railways at this time were getting a lot of abuse from the travelling public because of all the delays, and Dandridge felt that some suitable poster publicity would make them more understanding and tolerant of the disrupted services.

The slogan that Dandridge had thought of to use as a caption on the posters, was 'The Lines Behind the Front Line', but after some discussion he altered this to 'The Lines Behind The Lines'. A series of six photographic double royal posters was produced using this caption, but by far the best were two quad royal pictorials by Frank Mason. One was a dockyard scene with the caption 'Another Convoy is Discharged to the Lines Behind the Lines'. The second portrayed a steelworks and railway sidings with the caption, 'Unceasing Service On The Lines Behind The Lines'. Although all of these posters were published by the LNER they were issued under the British Railways heading.

The two quad royals were both reprinted and re-issued in 1941, but by this time the Germans had pushed our forces out of mainland Europe, in consequence of which we had no 'front line' to have lines behind. It was for this reason that the caption was changed in the reprinted posters.

The LNER was involved in the production of another classic Second World War poster, when in 1941 Bert Thomas was commissioned to design a pictorial poster to discourage unnecessary rail travel. Thomas was famous for his humorous cartoons and posters, and the slogan he used this time was 'Is Your Journey Really Necessary?'. This slogan was to be used extensively throughout the war on posters and press advertisements, and became a catchword for many years.

Throughout the war the Advertising Department was to find itself in the alien position of exhorting the public not to travel, or if you had to travel, 'Don't Take

Too Much Luggage' or 'Take your Own Food With You'. At one period in 1942 'Carry Your Own Cups And Glasses As Refreshment Rooms Are Often Short', was the plea on many posters. In the case of this last advertisement, the fact was that because they were in very short supply, cups and glasses were being stolen from the railway refreshment rooms in large numbers by the travelling public.

In March 1944 Cecil Dandridge was promoted to Passenger Manager (Southern Area) but he was to retain overall charge of the Advertising Department for the time being. May 1945 saw the end of the war in Europe, and by August of that year the Japanese had surrendered, bringing the Second World War to an end.

It was during August 1945 that it was announced that Cecil Dandridge was to relinquish the official post of Advertising Manager. No doubt it was felt that with the end of the war, the department would again need a manager's full-time attention. It must have been with some regret that Dandridge severed his connection with a job he had held so successfully for so many eventful years.

It was shortly confirmed that A.J. White was to succeed Dandridge with effect from 1 January 1946. White was to move from his post as Chief of LNER Police (Southern Area). He had, however, worked under Dandridge some years previous, as Commercial Agent.

White had taken over in difficult times, as wartime restrictions were to continue for many years even though the war was over. In the two years between his taking office and the coming of nationalisation in 1948, he did not have much opportunity to make any great impact in the job. He must, however, be given the credit for producing a loose leaf booklet that he entitled *The Manual Of Advertising Practice*. The manual set out in detail the standard format for all LNER letterpress posters, handbills, press advertisements and timetable posters.

Without a doubt, a major factor in the success of the LNER's advertising and publicity came from the continuity that had been provided by only having two Advertising Managers throughout most of the company's life. This was mentioned in an article in the last edition of the *LNER Magazine*, where A.J. White paid great tribute to both W.M. Teasdale and C.G. Dandridge.

In the first months of British Railways A.J. White designed the original British Railways Totem, and he retired from British Railways in November 1959. This chapter would not be complete without relating that Cecil Dandridge went on to become Chief Commercial Manager of British Railways Eastern Region, where for several years he was involved with rail journeys made by the royal family, and in 1950 he was made a Commander of the Victorian Order by Her Majesty the Queen. He retired in August 1955 after nearly fifty years in railway service, and died in November 1960 at the age of seventy.

Chapter Two

PICTORIAL POSTERS

After the grouping of the railways in 1923, the advertising styles of the four newly-formed companies took on a different outlook from their pre-grouping ancestors. Much of the bickering was over and there was now not quite such a competitive influence.

W.M. Teasdale, the LNER's Advertising Manager, had an eye for the more modernistic approach and was determined to set a high standard for the company's pictorial posters. From the beginning he was to provide a variety and quality that had rarely before been seen in the world of commercial art. He once referred to the pre-grouping companies pictorial posters as 'coloured bills' that were neither 'pictorial' nor 'posters'.

The LMS also started out to make something of a mark with their posters. They engaged Norman Wilkinson, a fine artist who had done a lot of work for the LNWR, to commission a group of Royal Academicians to produce a series of prestigious posters, but although these were of a high artistic standard, they on the whole seemed to lack something of the sparkle of the LNER's posters.

So far as the Great Western and Southern Railways were concerned, the output and quality of their pictorial posters were never to be quite in the same class as those of the LNER, although in later years they both came up with the occasional winner.

Teasdale called in artists such as Fred Taylor, Frank Mason, Frank Newbould, Tom Purvis and Austin Cooper among others, and soon had them working on commissions for the company. It was Austin Cooper that described in art terms the aims of these artists as being 'a kind of simplified realism'. Many other fine artists did work for the company, but it was the five mentioned artists that over the years formed the backbone of the LNER's poster design team.

It has been stated that the LNER paid some of its regular poster designers a retaining fee, but this was never the case. What actually happened was that for the first couple of years of the company's life, Teasdale commissioned each artist for each individual piece of work, but by 1926 the company was already acquiring a reputation for the quality of its pictorial posters and it was apparent that Teasdale was becoming rather worried that one or other of the main line companies might try to 'steal' one or more of his favoured artists.

Teasdale therefore decided to call a meeting at Kings Cross between Fred Taylor, Frank Mason, Frank Newbould, Tom Purvis and Austin Cooper. Teasdale put before them a proposal that he was prepared to offer each of them a guarantee that they would be given LNER commissions to a minimum agreed amount if, in return, they would undertake not to carry out any work for the other main line companies.

This agreement was to be for a three year period from 1927 and could be terminated by any of the artists giving three months notice in writing, but could not be broken by the company.

Teasdale advised that whilst he considered the five artists to form the nucleus of the company's poster designers, he reserved the right to commission any other artist that he wished. He also made it clear that in spite of any future artistic trends, he expected that their style of work should remain much as they had previously produced for the company.

All five artists readily agreed to Teasdale's proposals, although their annual guaranteed minimum commission fees varied considerably and was to be based on the approximate amount they had each received from the company during 1926.

The agreement with the five artists worked well for the first three year period. By the time that the agreement was due for renewal Dandridge had taken control of the Advertising Department and he approached the 'big five', as he called them, with an offer to renew for a further three-year period i.e. 1930, 1931 and 1932. His terms gave an approximate increase of 25% on the guaranteed minimum fees, which again varied between the artists.

At the lower end Frank Mason was to receive £35 for each double royal poster and £65 for a quad royal, whereas Fred Taylor, who was the highest paid, was to get £50 for double royals and £100 for a quad royal.

Again the three year agreement was very successful but, toward the end of the term, the acute depression of the early 1930s was beginning to make itself felt and Dandridge had to advise the 'big five' that he would not be able to renew their contracts, which expired at the end of 1932. He went on to say that although they would have no contract, he had every intention of using their services to the fullest extent that the current conditions would permit.

The great majority of the pictorial posters were of course advertising the holiday and tourist areas served by the company, and these posters were the result of a considerable amount of negotiation during the winter months between the representatives of each resort and the Advertising Manager.

For the LNER's first summer season of 1923, forty-five pictorial posters were produced, most of which were for holiday resorts, but over the years there were about sixty-five resorts that took part in the joint poster arrangements with the company. Some of the larger towns would require more than one poster but, taking an average year, there would be between seventy-five to a hundred different pictorials to produce not counting, of course, any of the LNER's own prestige posters.

The artists' fees and the cost of producing the poster were usually shared between the resort authority and the company, but it was the company that made all the arrangements, which included selecting the artist and having the poster printed.

From the artist's point of view, he would be asked by the Advertising Manager to visit the particular resort, where quite often he would make contact with the town's Publicity Officer in order to find which particular location would give the best results. It was also important to find out if there were any particular features that it would be desirable to emphasise.

The well-known poster artist J. Littlejohns was once quoted as saying that 'the first part of the problem is generally the most embarrassing. Some resorts are so unattractive to an artist he wonders why anyone could endure such a holiday. He is tempted to beautify in a manner that would constitute a fraud. If the place is unattractive, I look for distinctive features which mark it out from more or less similar places'.

It is a fact that Frank Sherwin was once sent to a Norfolk resort to produce a joint LNER-LMS poster. It was the middle of winter and the poster was for the following holiday season. Sherwin was back the next day saying that 'all he found was a beach with sand dunes sprouting the odd tuft of marram grass, and in an otherwise featureless landscape there was a deserted and semi-derelict tea hut, a scene, he said, he could not do a great deal with'.

Another very well-known artist, who shall have to remain anonymous, has recalled the time he was sent to a certain East Coast resort where he was to meet a representative of the local Publicity Department, who requested that the required poster should show the whole of the promenade, which happened to be some two miles long. Notwithstanding that particular problem the artist was particularly requested to leave out the very large hotel in the centre, as the owners had refused to join the local Chamber of Commerce.

Perhaps today we tend to look upon these surviving pictorial posters with a different eye, for they give an artistic impression of happier days gone by. However the one thing the artist had always to keep in mind was the fact that the object of the poster was primarily to 'sell' the resort, rather than the poster itself.

Teasdale had, with some justification, been pleased with the success of his department's pictorial posters and every year, from the company's formation up to his promotion to Assistant General Manager in 1927, he had arranged an informal exhibition of the current year's posters in the boardroom at Kings Cross.

These 'poster art' exhibitions as they became known had been well received but presumably the location was a bit restrictive, and when Cecil Dandridge took over the Department on 1 January 1928 he had much grander ideas. He lost no time in arranging with the New Burlington Art Galleries in London to hold an exhibition of the company's 1928 posters during March of that year.

One hundred and twenty-eight posters were exhibited, together with some of the LNER's booklet covers. As a guide to the exhibition, a small booklet was produced which listed the posters being shown. The last two pages of the guide gave an alphabetical list of the artists, and it was also pointed out that copies of the posters could be purchased at the galleries for 5*s* (25p) the quad royal size and 2*s* 6*d* (12½p) the double royal.

In order to get the maximum amount of publicity from the exhibition, Dandridge had invited some of the national press to the opening. Among the reports in the press the following day, both *The Times* and *Daily Telegraph* gave lengthy and favourable accounts of the display.

Dandridge's bold move to stage the exhibition in the New Burlington Galleries had, in publicity terms, paid off and in 1929 he repeated the exercise with another exhibition at the same venue. At the same time he arranged an exhibition at the company's offices at Waterloo Place Edinburgh.

Over the following years the poster exhibitions increased in number, 1934 seeing no less than thirteen in places as far apart as Aberdeen and Bournemouth.

1937 saw the last big London exhibition, once again at the New Burlington Galleries. It was opened by the Minister of Transport, and it was said that the audience at the opening was the largest ever seen at any similar event and included several of the LNER's Directors.

As we have seen, the majority of the company's pictorial posters were of the type produced jointly with the holiday resorts, these would of course be posted up in the spring of each year in the hope of attracting the prospective holidaymaker. At the end of the summer these would be promptly removed, as it was policy to replace posters fairly frequently in order to maintain interest.

Several of the larger LNER hotels held regular dinner dances throughout the season from October to May. In order to ensure that the ladies kept a cool head, they were provided with LNER fans.

For the autumn and winter a new set of posters would be produced, these would usually be some of the LNER's own 'prestige' posters which would probably advertise some of the company's services such as shipping, hotels, freight etc. Other subjects could be buildings of historic interest that were located on the company's system. It was here that Fred Taylor excelled with his skill at painting architectural subjects.

The very first pictorial poster produced by the LNER was, in fact, the quad royal of York Minster interior in which Fred Taylor made such a magnificent job of depicting the stained glass windows. Another very early prestige pictorial was the quad royal, 'Royal Border Bridge' by Frank Brangwyn R.A. In this instance Brangwyn not only did the design but carried out a major part of the lithographic art work for the poster, which in those days was a highly skilled process involving faithfully copying the original design onto a series of special lithographic stones.

It is of interest to note that although the LMS made much of their poster scheme employing Royal Academicians, they were in fact just 'pipped to the post' when Teasdale commissioned Brangwyn who was an R.A. and it was always something of a boast that the LNER were the first railway to commission a Royal Academician to design a poster.

One of the most well-known resort posters ever designed must have been John Hassall's 'Skegness Is So Bracing', showing the jolly fisherman prancing along the seashore. This poster was of course originally designed for the Great Northern Railway, one of the LNER's constituents. Perhaps it is not quite so well known

YORK ON THE TRACK OF THE FLYING SCOTSMAN

LONDON & NORTH EASTERN RAILWAY OF ENGLAND AND SCOTLAND

Fred Taylor must have painted more of York's old buildings than any other poster artist. This quad royal of St Williams College was published in 1928. The slogan 'On the Track of the Flying Scotsman' was often used by the LNER and has, in fact, been resurrected by today's Great North Eastern Railway.

that around 1930 Hassall was asked to re-design the poster, and in its revised form, Hassall removed the clouds from the sky and provided Skegness with a pier.

During the main productive years for the company's pictorial posters, which were between 1923-1940, many artists were commissioned, some of whom only ever designed one or two posters for the LNER. There were, however, many names other than the 'big five' that were to appear year after year, amongst the more well known being H.G. Gawthorn, Doris Zinkeisen, and to a lesser extent her sister Anna, Montague Black, Arthur C. Michael and Bert Thomas, and of course there were many more.

Any discussion about LNER pictorial posters will, however, inevitably return to the 'big five' who during the 1930s produced amongst others a number of double royal posters in series, usually of six. There was 'Old World Market Places' by Austin Cooper, for which he was paid £222 for the set. Cooper also produced several other series, including 'The Birth Places Of Musicians', 'Famous Authors' and 'Passengers of the Past'. It is strange that in one of the posters in this last mentioned set, Cooper has depicted a character that is a mirror image of Cecil Dandridge.

GARAGE YOUR CAR AT THE STATION

Special terms for
SEASON TICKET
HOLDERS

CONVENIENCE SECURITY
LOW RENTALS

Full particulars from Station Master

Another simple message from Frank Newbould. The provision of lock-up garages at stations was a little known service, and one wonders if any of the garages survive today.

Another series of six double royals was entitled *Passengers of the Past*. They were produced in 1929 by Austin Cooper. The reader may like to compare the small bowler-hatted figure on the right with the picture of Cecil Dandridge at Kings Cross.

THE TYNE

MODERN EQUIPMENT FOR HEAVIEST SHIPMENTS
L·N·E·R DOCKS ARE THE LARGEST FOR COAL
EXPORTING IN THE WORLD
REGULAR SAILINGS TO NORTHERN EUROPE
ADJACENT HOLIDAY RESORTS – WHITLEY BAY TYNEMOUTH AND SOUTH SHIELDS

LONDON AND NORTH EASTERN RAILWAY

The East Coast is endowed with several large rivers, upon which was sited a great deal of industry. In 1932 Frank Mason was asked to design a set of four quad royal posters to publicise the activities centered around these rivers. He gave the posters a rather sombre treatment, and 'The Tyne' shown here is typical of all four.

Frank Mason designed a set of six 'Havens And Harbours', all East Coast of course. He also produced a series on 'Inshore Fishermen'. It was unusual to produce quad royals in series, but Mason designed a set of four very fine posters entitled 'Famous Rivers of Commerce' for which his fee was £260 in 1931.

In 1930 Frank Newbould designed a series of six double royals entitled 'East Coast Types', of which number five, 'The Deck Chair Man', and number six, 'The Donkey Boy', became classics of their day.

For the 1936 holiday season, Tom Purvis produced a series of double royals for Clacton-on-Sea, Lowestoft, Skegness, Scarborough, Robin Hood's Bay and Bamburgh. The six posters were extremely cleverly designed so that when displayed as a set side-by-side they formed a continuous strip of coastline. They could, however, be displayed individually and would give a true representation of the seafront of each particular resort.

1934 saw the Advertising Department experimenting with a series of photo-graphic posters. Some of these were produced by having a set made up to represent the inside of a compartment with two passengers inside to give an 'out of the carriage window' view of a particular resort. The whole effect was rather dismal and was only used for one or two seasons.

In marked contrast to the photographic posters, some superb designs were produced to advertise the streamline train services of the late 1930s. 'The Silver Jubilee' by Frank Newbould must rank among his best. There is no doubt that some of the quality of this particular poster must be attributed to the lithographic printers who were Sanders, Philips & Co. but better known as the Baynard Press. Baynard had built up a very high reputation for their quality printing and, in the case of Newbould's 'Silver Jubilee', they made a fine job of the lithographic reproduction.

1937 saw some fine double royals being produced to advertise the Scarborough Flyer and the new West Riding Limited. These posters, together with a poster for the Coronation published the following year, were designed by Shep. The produc-tion of these posters was something of a break with normal practice, in that Dandridge again went to the Baynard Press, but Baynard's carried out both the design and printing, Shep being the signature of J.C.M. Shepard who was Head of Baynard's design studio.

Perhaps a matter of interest is that it seems that when the Baynard Press Studios produced artwork, Baynard's retained the copyright for any purpose other than the purpose for which the artwork was commissioned.

Some of the last pictorials to appear before the start of the Second World War were in conjunction with the 'Meet The Sun On The East Coast' campaign that had been launched by Dandridge on 3 April 1939. This was to be a major effort to bring more holiday traffic to the East Coast resorts, at the same time that the Southern Railway's Advertising Manager, Cuthbert Grasemann, was pushing the slogan 'Go South For Sunshine'.

It was shortly after the end of the Second World War, that a new artist to the LNER was requested to discuss the possibility of repainting to double royal size a picture he had previously had on exhibition. The picture was of an old watermill just on the Essex border. The artist readily accepted the commission and it was in this way that the late Terence Cuneo said he was enrolled into railway poster work.

After completing the Essex Mill poster, Cuneo was asked to visit the LNER locomotive works at Doncaster, where one of the streamlined A4 locomotives was being overhauled and repainted in peacetime livery. This visit ultimately resulted in what must arguably be one of the all-time greats in railway posters. The poster was, of course, the quad royal 'Giants Refreshed'.

GIANTS REFRESHED
"PACIFICS" IN THE LNER LOCOMOTIVE WORKS, DONCASTER

It is doubtful if this poster needs any description. Terence Cuneo was commissioned by the LNER in 1947 and a few of the posters were printed with the LNER caption shown. However natonalisation came about and many more of the posters were printed with a new British Railways caption.

It is certain the poster needs no description here. However what may not be realised is that there were two versions of the poster, one that was obviously printed for the LNER with the caption 'Giants Refreshed, Pacifics In The LNER Locomotive Works' Doncaster'. The other version has the caption 'Giants Refreshed, Pacifics In The Doncaster Locomotive Works'. This second version has the British Railways Totem.

Cuneo was also commissioned by the LNER to produce another quad royal prestige pictorial. This was captioned 'Royal Border Bridge', and was a magnificent picture of an LNER freight train crossing the bridge at Berwick. Unfortunately Cuneo completed the picture just at the time of nationalisation, and the poster was printed with a British Railways caption.

We have seen that the Advertising Department had offices at York and Edinburgh as well as London. It was the rule however that pictorial posters were always produced under the direct control of the Advertising Manager at London.

Although the company had its own large printing works at Stratford Market, they did not have the facilities for producing large coloured lithographic posters and these were always put up for tender by such firms as Waterlow & Sons, Sanders, Philips & Co. (the Baynard Press) Ben Johnson & Co., The Dangerfield Printing Co., Jordison & Co., the Haycock Press, Chorley & Pickersgill, Adams Bros & Shardlow and McCorquodale & Co.

For the railway company the pictorial poster was a relatively cheap form of advertising, bearing in mind that the cost of resort posters was shared with the particular resort, and the postboards were in the main on company premises. It has often been asked if the cost of these posters was justified in terms of increased passengers, and this question was almost impossible to answer categorically.

The fact that, year after year, the resorts came back to renew their arrangements with the company was proof enough that at least they were convinced of the efficacy of the pictorial poster. There was another plus so far as the company was concerned, and that was that part of the agreement with each resort was that every enquiry received by the resorts would be passed on to the company to be followed up by advising of train travel details. Taking 1930 as a good example, no fewer than 75,000 enquiries were dealt with from the sixty-five resorts involved that year.

There was another not insignificant factor relating to the pictorial poster, and in this respect Francis Goodricke, the Assistant Advertising Manager was once quoted as saying 'If for a moment it could be supposed that pictorial posters had no advertising value, their decorative effect alone would justify their production'. It was a little-known fact that the railway companies relied upon the brightly coloured pictorials to cover up some parts of their stations that were almost always in dire need of redecoration.

It must in fairness be said that in the case of railway pictorial posters, it was not nationalisation that changed the scene, for although they were difficult times, many fine posters were produced in the early days of British Railways.

It was the so called 'March of Progress' that brought modern and cheaper photographic methods of production, that sadly ensured that whilst we waited for our trains, we would no longer have the great pleasure of seeing posters produced by such fine artists as Fred Taylor, Frank Newbould, Frank Mason, Terence Cuneo and all the others who over many years kept the LNER in the forefront of pictorial publicity.

Chapter Three

BOOKS
AND BOOKLETS

There can be little doubt that of the four main line companies, the LNER led the way in the production of pictorial posters. When it came to the production of books and booklets, it must with some certainty be agreed that the Great Western was well ahead of the others both in quantity as well as quality.

So far as the LNER was concerned, W.M. Teasdale was known to be of the opinion that there were more than enough travel publications on the market. His successor, Cecil Dandridge, was little more enthusiastic, being quoted on at least one occasion as saying that he felt the general public were only mildly interested in travel literature.

It is a fact, however, that the LNER's Advertising Department, under the very able management of these two gentlemen, did produce a more than adequate selection of books and booklets, the great majority of which dealt with holiday and leisure interests.

In many of the LNER's publications, one will often find one page devoted to listing the currently available LNER literature. It is possible to gain much information from looking through these pages, but for anyone wishing to carry out a comprehensive study of the company's publications, it should be noted that these lists can be somewhat misleading.

It has been stated on good authority that the Advertising Department was run on very informal lines and, with some of the publications being dealt with by the York or Edinburgh offices as well as at London, it is perhaps understandable that things were not recorded as present-day researchers would have wished.

Prior to the amalgamation in 1923, the LNER's constituent companies had been publishing various holiday and tourist booklets. Understandably there was to be a certain overlap during the first months of the new company's existence. One example of this was the set of booklets entitled 'The Holiday Series', which were a slightly modified version of a series previously published by the North Eastern.

There were twenty titles in the 1923 Holiday Series, each describing a particular holiday area served by the LNER. The covers of the booklets were a rather drab grey, and illustrated with charcoal sketches by Frank Mason. In most cases the booklets were designed to be folded vertically down the centre to enable them to be easily carried in the pocket

For 1924 the Holiday Series booklets had completely re-designed covers by Freda Lingstrom, these consisted of a small central illustration in addition to which was a rather unusual design of the company's initials in the bottom corner. An additional title was added to the series this year, and in some cases the text was re-written.

For 1925 the Holiday Series remained much as the previous year, but with the addition of another title, bringing the total to twenty-two. 1926 saw the Series reduced to twelve titles which was due to some of the areas being combined into single booklets, with consequent revision of the text.

Thirteen titles were available in 1928 and these were given new covers again by Freda Lingstrom, but by the end of the year all but three of the booklets went out of print. The remaining three booklets were still available in 1929 but the Series came to an end in 1930.

Another publication produced during the first year of amalgamation, was *Holiday Suggestions*, a booklet of some seventy-two pages with a cover designed by Lillian Hocknell. It covered nearly seventy holiday resorts on the LNER's system between the Thames in the south to the Moray Firth in the north. This free booklet was available up to the end of 1925, but for 1926 the title was shortened to *Holidays*. It was recorded that no less than 200,000 copies of this publication were issued in 1926.

Running parallel to *Holiday Suggestions* was a set of booklets published under the general title of *Lodgings and Hotels Guide*. For the first year (1923) there were four volumes, these were 'Eastern Counties', 'North Eastern Counties', 'Scotland', and 'Other Districts Reached By The LNER'.

These guides were made up of descriptive text and photographs, with classified advertisements for hotels, boarding houses etc. The guides ran to around 300 pages each, and the *Railway Gazette* in reviewing the books said: 'These booklets contain a vast amount of information and will be of the greatest help to prospective pleasure seekers'.

From 1924 to 1928 the title of the guides was changed to *Apartments and Hotels Guide*, and the volume dealing with 'Other Districts Reached By The LNER' was

The 'Durham County' booklet shown here is
one of the then newly designed 1924 *Holidays*
series. The 'East Anglia' booklet is also from
the same series, but had again been re-designed
and dates from around 1928. Both artwork
covers are by Freda Lingstrom.

The LNER *Holiday Handbook* became known by the Advertising Department as their 'heavyweight' and was always number one on the list of publications. Shown here is the very first edition of 1929.

dropped. However, around 1927 a booklet dealing with the Isle of Skye was published. Like most of the LNER's publications, the guides were issued free, but it is known that the cost of production was just about covered by the income from advertisers.

It was soon after taking over the Advertising Department, that Cecil Dandridge decided to bring the LNER into line with the other main line companies, in publishing a more prestigious 'all line' holiday guide. In this he knew he was behind the Southern Railway whose *Hints for Holidays* had previously been published by the London & South Western Railway.

The Great Western could boast that their *Holiday Haunts* was on sale for 1d as early as 1906, although by 1911 the price had risen to 6d (2½p), which became the standard price fixed by all companies up to 1940.

What became known in the Advertising Department as 'our heavyweight' was launched in April 1929, with the official title of *The Holiday Handbook*. This first mammoth edition which, like its rivals, sold for 6d (2½p), ran to some 1,140 pages, and was said to be the largest holiday guide ever published.

Press advertisements for the *Holiday Handbook* were always placed in April. This is the advertisement for the 1930 edition.

The response to the new publication took Dandridge by surprise, when within seventeen days of being put on sale, the first impression of 50,000 copies was sold out, and he had to order an immediate reprint of a further 50,000 copies.

The re-printed edition was of course identical to the original, except that rather strangely it was printed with the words 'second edition' on the front cover, which can today be rather confusing bearing in mind that no year of publication appears on the book.

The *Holiday Handbook* followed much the same format as its competitors in giving descriptions of most of the holiday resorts served by the LNER, together with a huge number of advertisements in classified and display form.

The book was divided into four sections dealing with The Eastern Counties, Yorkshire, Northumberland, Durham and The Lake District, and Scotland. From the first edition until 1936, each section had its pages numbered independently but with a separate suffix letter i.e. 'a' after the page numbers in the Eastern Counties section, 'b' for the Yorkshire pages and so on. The reason for this was that for several years, each section of the Handbook could be obtained free as a separate booklet. From 1937 on, the pages were numbered continuously and without the suffixes. Each section was printed by a separate printer, and in the early years there were at least five printing companies involved in its production.

No doubt pleased with the success of the first year of the new book, Dandridge ordered 150,000 copies for the 1930 (third edition), but on this occasion he seems to have been somewhat overconfident, for when it came to preparing the 1931 edition, he reported to the Passenger Managers Committee, 'that because of the depressed state of trade, an appreciable number of the 1930 edition were still available'. He advised that instead of issuing a new book for 1931 he intended to have the existing books re-bound in new green covers and use errata slips as necessary. This was in fact how the 1931 Handbook was produced.

The Advertising Department under both Teasdale and Dandridge, always tried to aim at a rather high class image, and the *Holiday Handbook* was no exception. From the first edition in 1929 until the 1936 edition, the covers were rather plain. The cover for the 1936 book was designed by Frank Newbould but was a rather

---

GREAT YARMOUTH
AND
GORLESTON-ON-SEA
FOR
HEALTHFUL—HAPPY—HOLIDAYS

Please send an ILLUSTRATED GUIDE of GREAT YARMOUTH and GORLESTON to

Name..
(Mr., Mrs., or Miss)

Address..

....

L.N.E.R.

Each year many of the larger resorts paid to have small slips bound into the *Holiday Handbook*. These could be completed and sent to the particular resort for more information to be forwarded.

Opposite: 1947 saw things trying to get back to pre-war standards, and this double royal announces 'back again' the *Holiday Handbook*. One thing has changed, however: the price had doubled to 1s (5p) as indeed did the other companies' guides.

Left: By 1936 the cover of the *Holiday Handbook* was beginning to change, although still very sober by other companies' standards.

subdued example of his work. The covers for the 1937 and 1938 editions sported some holiday scenes and were much more in keeping with the purpose of the book.

It was probably not realised at the time, but the public must have wondered how it was that every year all four main line companies holiday guides appeared on the bookstalls on exactly the same date. This of course was negotiated and precisely agreed by the companies' every year.

There were of course no *Holiday Handbooks* after 1940, and it was to be 1947 before the *Handbook* made its reappearance. By then its price had doubled to 1s (5p) for which one received 656 pages. The 1947 edition was to be the last LNER *Holiday Handbook*, and two of its three sections were still being printed by two of the original printers, who were Knapp, Drewett & Son, and Chorley & Pickersgill.

In 1925 the LNER introduced a booklet having the somewhat misleading title of *Holiday Camps On The LNER*. One would have been forgiven for thinking that

here was a booklet listing holiday camps on the system, but of course this was some years from the birth of the holiday camp that we know today.

The booklet, which had some 120 pages, listed camping sites and youth hostels that could be reached by the LNER. It was published for four years but, through apparent lack of interest, it was dropped in 1929.

When the LNER pioneered the 'Camping Coach' in 1933, the booklet was re-introduced the following year. It was completely revised to include full details of the Camping Coaches and the title was revised to *Camping Holidays*. With occasional updating, the booklet was available up to 1940.

Another publication that was carried over from pre-grouping days was *On Either Side*. This was a booklet designed, in the company's words: 'depicting and describing features of interest to be seen from the train'. The original booklet had been published by the Great Northern Railway, and the first (1923) LNER edition was a straightforward reprint with a change of company name.

This London-Scotland edition of *On Either Side* was published in 1935 with this superb cover design by Bryan DeGrineau.

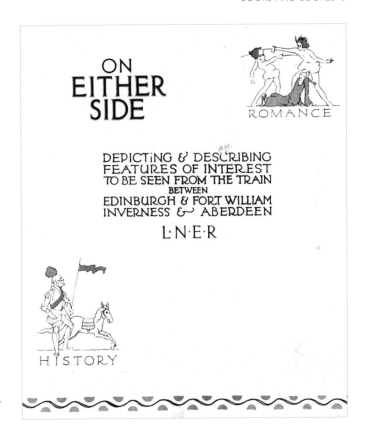

On Either Side This is a copy of the Scotland only edition of 1924. A not very inspiring cover by Freda Lingstrom.

On Either Side, which incidentally must have been the longest running publication, was primarily a straight line strip map of the LNER main line, giving stations and mileages. There was also some text and photographs which described various places of interest to be seen on the route.

The first edition described the route between Kings Cross and Edinburgh, and the plain cover was only half the width of the booklet, which was designed to be kept folded in half to facilitate being carried in one's pocket.

Around the middle of 1924 another edition of *On Either Side* was published, this edition dealing with lines in Scotland. The cover this time was full width with some rather out of keeping artwork by Freda Lingstrom. This sole edition for Scotland had some thirty-eight pages and was only published for one year, when it was decided to incorporate both booklets into one new edition.

The basic format of the new edition was much as before, but now ran to seventy-five pages. Because of the increased thickness of the booklet and in order to be able to fold it in half, it meant that the back cover had to be considerably wider than the front in order to get the edges to meet when folded.

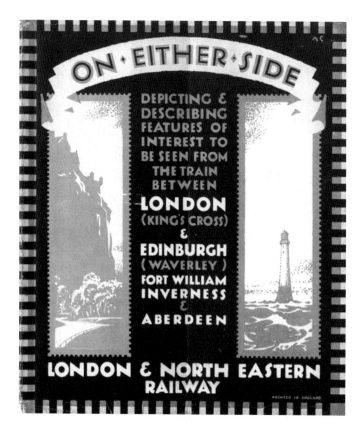

This comprehensive edition of *On Either Side* is thought to have been first put on sale at the British Empire Exhibition of 1925. Cover by Austin Cooper.

The East Anglian edition of *On Either Side* was published in 1932 with a somewhat complicated cover design by Frank Newbould for which his fee was £33 5s 0d (£33.25).

The colourful cover of the new edition was by Austin Cooper, and was to be used up to around 1935, although during this time there was some minor modifications to the contents. It was during the currency of the Austin Cooper edition that the recession took hold, and for that reason the company started to make a charge for the booklet, which up to that time had been free.

From some time in 1931 the price of 3d (1½p) was overprinted on the cover. Whether charging for the booklet had any effect on the numbers issued, or whether the finances of the company improved, the charge was dropped from the end of 1933.

Feeling there was a need for an East Anglian edition of *On Either Side*, such a booklet was published on 1 March 1932. The format was as before but covered the lines between London (Liverpool St) and the East Anglian resorts.

This new booklet had forty-two pages and the rather complicated but striking cover was by Frank Newbould for which he was paid £33 5s 0d (£33.25). At the time a charge of 3d was also made for this booklet up to 1933, but from then until this edition went out of print in 1938, it was issued free.

1935 saw a new edition of the London-Scotland booklet, with some revision of the text and some new photographs. In places, the strip map proudly indicated where the line had been equipped with 'modern electric signalling'. This edition was also given a new cover by Bryan DeGrineau, who was an excellent artist who unfortunately did little work for the LNER.

After only a year of the Bryan DeGrineau design, and because of the introduction of the

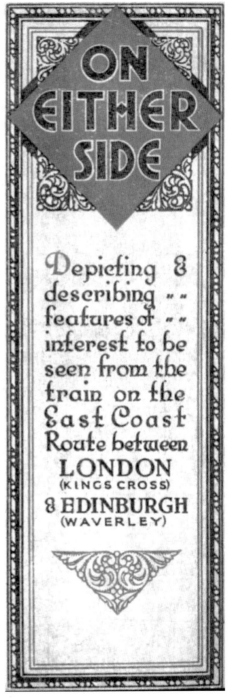

Of 1923 vintage, this was the first of the *On Either Side* booklets to carry the LNER name. However it is thought to be a reprint of the earlier Great Northern design with name amendments.

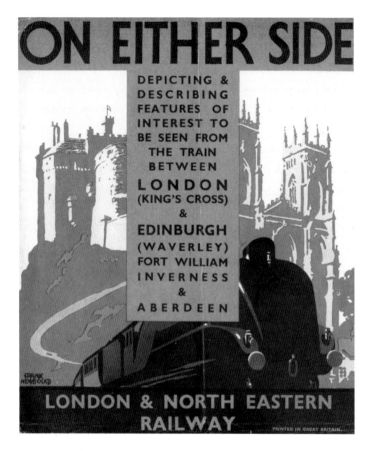

The last edition of *On Either Side* was published in 1936 with a cover by Frank Newbould. The content was late revised but the cover retained.

new A4 Streamliners, it was thought that a new edition of the London–Scotland *On The Line* should be published to reflect the new streamline era. To this end, 1936 saw Frank Newbould producing a striking new cover in orange, blue, yellow and black. The design depicted one of the new A4s against a background scene of London and Edinburgh. Although there was to be further revisions of the content up to 1939, this was to be the final cover design of the booklet, which was withdrawn shortly after the outbreak of war.

There must have been a fairly large stock of the pre-war edition of *On Either Side* remaining, as it was re-introduced shortly after the war ended. A charge of 1s (5p) per copy was made, but of course by this time much of the text was out of date. However the booklets were sold with an adhesive label on the cover advising that: 'This publication was issued in 1939, and the references to high speed trains, cheap tickets and holiday literature at the end of the book are no longer correct. The booklet continues to serve its main purpose of describing the principal features of interest along the East Coast Route'.

In the late 1920s, rambling was becoming an increasingly popular pastime and, with this in mind, the LNER published in September 1930 three sets of cards entitled *Walks Round London*. The cards, which covered rambles in Essex, Herts and Buckinghamshire, could be purchased singularly for 1*d* (½p) each or as a set at 1*s* (5p) per set. In 1932 three more sets were published covering rambles in Edinburgh District, Glasgow District and Norwich and District.

Although many sets of the cards were sold, they were slowly phased out, and by 1937 only the Glasgow and Edinburgh sets were available. The reason that the cards were phased out was in the main due to the introduction in March 1932 of the first two of the popular Rambles Booklets.

The first two booklets were *Rambles In Essex* and *Rambles in Hertfordshire*, and these set the pattern for all of the subsequent booklets in the series. The booklets had around seventy pages each and were written by authors known for their knowledge of the particular area.

Each ramble was described in the text and was complemented with a small map. Mileages were given and in some cases details of various cheap tickets that were available to the station concerned. All of the booklets, which were sold for 6*d* (2½p) each, followed a similar pattern, with colourful artwork covers.

By 1940 there were as many as seventeen different booklets in the *Rambles* series. Shown here and overleaf are just a few of varying ages.

RAMBLES IN SUFFOLK

PRICE SIXPENCE

LONDON AND NORTH EASTERN RAILWAY

RAMBLES
IN
EPPING FOREST
PRICE SIXPENCE
LONDON AND NORTH EASTERN RAILWAY

RAMBLES
IN
BUCKINGHAMSHIRE
PRICE SIXPENCE
LONDON AND NORTH EASTERN RAILWAY

**RAMBLES ON THE
YORKSHIRE COAST AND MOORS**
By JOHN HORNBY   Price Sixpence
LONDON AND NORTH EASTERN RAILWAY

RAMBLES
IN
THE CHILTERNS
PRICE SIXPENCE
LONDON AND NORTH EASTERN RAILWAY

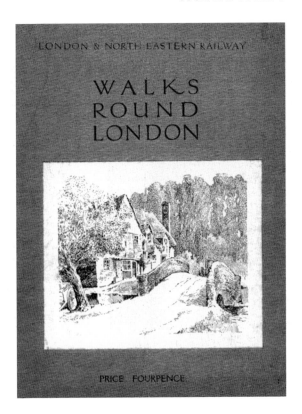

This *Walks Round London* booklet was published around 1925 and was almost certainly a reprint of an earlier pre-LNER edition.

All of the rambling publications had in fact been preceded as far back as 1923, by a booklet entitled *Walks Round London*. This publication was followed with *Walking and Cycling Tours in the Manchester District* (1925), *Walking Tours in the Edinburgh District* (1926) and *Walking Tours in the Glasgow District* in 1927, all of which were sale publications at 6*d* (2½p) each.

The Manchester booklet ran to several editions, and in 1935 the format was changed to bring it into line with the main 'Rambles' series, which by that date had become well established. The Edinburgh booklet went out of print in 1932 and the Glasgow edition was terminated in 1934. Some of the main 'Rambles' series were revised and by 1940 there were around seventeen booklets available, some even being reprinted after nationalisation.

The acquisition of several bus companies by the LNER in the late 1920s prompted the publication in 1932 of three booklets under the general title of 'New Ways For British Holidays'. These booklets, dealing with East Anglia, Yorkshire, and Scotland, gave details of bus and train services together with an accommodation list for each area. Two more booklets were shortly added to the set, and there was a general change in the subtitles to East Anglia, Lincolnshire and the Dukeries,

There were, altogether, four editions of the *Flying Scotsman* booklet – here we see the 1925 first edition with 4472 on the cover and the 1931 fourth edition with a somewhat stylized Locomotive 10000.

Yorkshire Coast, Yorkshire Dales, and Northumberland and Durham. The series were available until May 1937, when the general title was changed to 'Railway and Roadway Holidays'. Last year of publication was 1938.

Once again going back to the early days of the company, and to the Railway Centenary in particular, the LNER published a 130-page booklet entitled *The Flying Scotsman*. The booklet, which had card covers sporting a colourful picture of the train by H.G. Gawthorn, was sold for 1s (5p) per copy, which at that time was not exactly cheap, but was about par with the other companies similar publications.

The booklet gave a full history of the train, together with a description of the journey from London to Scotland. *The Flying Scotsman* was to run to four editions, the last of which was published in 1931 with a striking illustration of *Locomotive 10000* on the cover. This edition was to remain available up to 1937, by which time it was becoming a little out of date in the 'streamline' era, and it went out of print in favour of a new book by Cecil J. Allen.

Allen's new book, entitled *The Coronation and Other Famous LNER Trains*, was published on 1 June 1937 by Ivor Nicholson & Watson and its 176 pages sold for 1s. Although not published by the LNER, the book seems to have been 'adopted' by the company as an official publication, and was available up to 1940.

The Coronation and Other Famous LNER Trains was an 'adopted' booklet that was actually published by Nicholson & Watson. The booklet was, however, widely advertised by the LNER.

LOCOMOTIVES OF THE L.N.E.R.
PAST AND PRESENT.

Three-cylinder Pacific Type Express Locomotive No. 4476, "Royal Lancer," London & North Eastern Ry.   (*See description other side.*)
Published with the Authority of the London & North Eastern Railway by The Locomotive Publishing Co., Ltd., London.
PRICE ONE SHILLING.

Locomotives of the LNER Past and Present was another adopted boolet. This is the 1929 first edition.

Mention must also be made of another 'adopted' booklet, which was *Locomotives of the LNER Past and Present*. The booklet of some forty-eight pages, was first published by the Locomotive Publishing Co. in 1929, and sold for 1*s* (5p). Like its title suggests, it gave a great deal of technical information on LNER locomotives both old and new. Revised editions were published in 1935 and 1938, but this latter edition was renamed *LNER Locomotives*.

In 1944, the late George Dow, who was at that time Press and Public Relations Officer for the LNER, wrote the first of a series of four booklets to commemorate the railway companies that formed part of the history of the LNER.

The first of these booklets was *The Story Of The West Highland*, which went to a second, enlarged, edition in 1947. The second booklet in the series was *The First Railway In Norfolk*, and this also went to a second enlarged edition in 1947. The third booklet was *The First Railway Between Manchester And Sheffield* and was published in 1945. The fourth and last was published in 1946 with the title *The First Railway Across The Border*. These booklets were all sold at between 1*s* and 3*s* 6*d* (17½p) each.

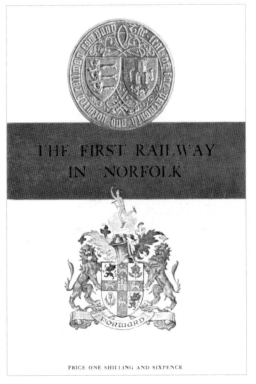 

Pictured here are two of the booklets written by George Dow, which were published at the time he was Press and Public Relations Officer of the LNER.

It is not possible to detail all of the LNER's books in this review. There was *A Round Of Golf on The LNER* that was first published in 1924 and went out of print in 1928. This title was 'dusted off' and re-published in 1938. A similar situation was *Salmon And Trout Rivers served By The LNER*, which was only available for a couple of years, but the title was resurrected by another author in 1937 and this was being sold up to 1940.

There were several booklets on Scottish and Continental travel, and one must not forget that many publications were also printed in two or three languages. Annual pocket-sized booklets were issued listing the many agricultural shows and markets, but from 1932 these were published jointly by the four companies. The LNER ports, docks and freight services also had booklets giving their main features.

The Advertising Department presumably thought that it would be a good idea to get some sense of order with the company's publications and it was about the time of the publication of the first *Holiday Handbook* (1929) that most of the more important travel publications were given a publication, or what the Advertising

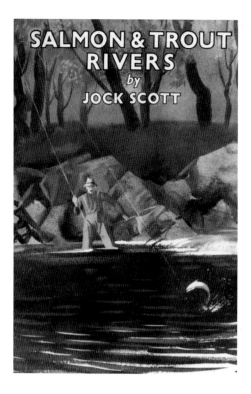

Salmon and Trout Rivers was a title that had previously been used for an earlier publication. In 1937 the title was re-used in a completely new book that remained on sale up to 1940.

Department called a 'Registered Number'. This was printed on the bottom left-hand corner of the front cover. The purpose of this number was mainly to enable staff to recognise and re-order new stocks of the publications, rather than to quote some of the more lengthy titles.

One would imagine that this would be of great help to present-day research, but the fact is that with the provision of new publications and the phasing out of old literature, the Registered Numbers very often did not remain constant on a year by year basis. Taking the booklet *Belgium Via Harwich* as an example, this was numbered 20 in 1929 and in subsequent years became 19, 26, 31, 37 and 30 up to 1934.

There were however several publications that did retain the same number, the *Holiday Handbook* was always number 1, the Sectional Holiday Guides also retained the same numbers.

Another complication, although perhaps to a lesser extent, is that those publications that were published jointly with the LMS, were printed with the LNER number when issued by that company, but although identical in all other respects the number was omitted on those copies issued by the LMS.

Over the years there were several publications that, generally speaking, were not available to the general public. *Ports of the London & North Eastern Railway* was one

PORTS

of the

LONDON & NORTH EASTERN RAILWAY

1934

Shown here are the two known Fred Taylor 'Sketchbooks'. There may well have been others in the series but, along with *Ports of the LNER*, they were among other books that were not generally advertised as being available to the public.

HOLLAND
BELGIUM
VIA
HARWICH

BY LEWIS HIND
& FRED TAYLOR R.I

YORKSHIRE

A SKETCH BOOK BY
FRED TAYLOR, R.I.

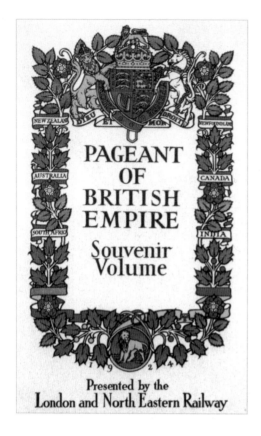

Pageant of British Empire. This large book, which measured 310mm x 410mm, was surely the most exotic book that the LNER was involved with and was for special presentation only.

example, being first published in 1927 and thereafter revised annually. The book gave details of the ports and harbours that the company owned or was associated with.

There were at least two printed 'sketchbooks' by Fred Taylor. These were *Yorkshire a Sketchbook by Fred Taylor RI*, and *Holland Belgium via Harwich*, which in addition to Fred Taylor's sketches, contained text by Lewis Hind.

These 'sketchbooks' ran to forty-two pages and thirty pages respectively and both are thought to be of around 1924 vintage. None of these books appear to have been advertised, so it must be assumed that they were for special presentation. There can be no doubt that the most splendid book ever associated with the LNER was a very large volume that was superbly produced by Fleetway Press. The book was printed in 1924 with the title *Pageant of British Empire*. It was a souvenir book that was in celebration of the pageant that was held at the British Empire Exhibition.

The book contained some fifty-five pages of reproductions of paintings by Frank Brangwyn RA, Spencer Pryse and Macdonald Gill, and was in full colour throughout. The hard cover, which had a glassine wrapper was, in addition to the

By Rail To Victory was a hard cover book that was to be the last major publication before nationalisation. It was published in 1947 and sold for 7s 6d (37½p). The artwork dust wrapper was by John Bee.

title and other illustrations, boldly printed with the fact that it was, 'Presented by the London and North Eastern Railway'.

One of the preliminary pages gives some brief details of the LNER's shipping and docks services. It would seem that the purpose of the book was as a special presentation to a visiting dignitary who may be persuaded into using the company's services.

The last major publication produced by the LNER was *By Rail to Victory*. This was a hardbound book telling the story of the LNER in the Second World War. Written by Norman Crump, the book was of some 196 pages and sold for 7*s* 6*d* (37½p) and was complete with an artwork wrapper by John Bee.

By the time that *By Rail to Victory* was published, nationalisation of the company seemed to be a forgone conclusion and, in the foreword to the book, Sir Ronald Matthews, who was at that time chairman of the LNER said, 'We have all of us learnt much from these years of hardship and danger, but the greatest lesson of all is this, that whatever the future may have in store for British railways, the team spirit of the LNER is something far too precious to be allowed to die'.

Chapter Four

LETTERPRESS POSTERS, HANDBILLS, FOLDERS AND PRESS ADVERTISEMENTS

Letterpress Posters

The letterpress poster was probably the cheapest form of general advertising available to the company. They could be produced at very short notice with the minimum of preparation, a good percentage actually being printed at the LNER Printing Works. They cost very little to produce, and even less to display on the company's own billboards, where they were more often than not 'posted' by the station staff.

The pre-grouping companies letterpress posters had for years contained as much information as it was possible to get on the 'bill'. Not only were they overcrowded with information but they were printed in as many different typefaces as the printers could muster. This was something that W.M. Teasdale was going to change.

Shortly after taking office, Teasdale, giving a lecture on advertising, said: 'letterpress bills can be read quickly if there is little to read, therefore reduce the message'. He went on to say 'Harwich For The Continent', is easier to read and remember than The LNER Company's Magnificent Royal Mail Steamers Leave Harwich For Antwerp and The Hook of Holland Each Weekday'. This has shown that simplicity is what is wanted, but it has not been easy to break the customs of generations.

In December 1928 Cecil Dandridge, who by then had taken over the Advertising Department, launched an innovative type of poster that he referred to as his 'Varieties poster'. The format was almost identical to the small theatrical poster of the period, being printed with a small pictorial heading by Corona Studios. This showed the facades of the LNER stations at Marylebone, Kings Cross and Liverpool St, with the overwritten title 'LNER VARIETY PROGRAMME'.

SALT·BURN·BY·THE·SEA

Illustrated Booklet free from the Clerk
to the Urban District Council Saltburn
or any L·N·E·R Enquiry Office.

1. A double royal poster by Frank Mason. This one was a 'one off' for Saltburn and was published in 1928.

2. Of 1926 vintage, this poster was one of a series of six with the series title *Sentinels of Britain's Beauty*. The set was designed by Frank Mason and this example asks that you remember Cruden Bay district for your holidays.

3. A double royal by A.R. Thompson, which was one of a series produced in 1930 to impress the comfort of LNER trains.

4. Bert Thomas produced the design for this poster in 1934. Using an Arabian Nights theme that had been used the year before, the caption asks that you let the LNER be your Sinbad to carry your load. Bert Thomas was later to design many of the Second World War posters.

LINCOLN

ON THE
LONDON & NORTH EASTERN RAILWAY
OF ENGLAND AND SCOTLAND

For Travel Information and Illustrated Literature apply to
Principal Tourist Agencies

5. Published in 1929, this double royal is by Fred Taylor. With this particular caption, it was probably printed for display abroad.

DOVERCOURT
IT'S QUICKER BY RAIL

6. From time to time the artistic Zinkeisen sisters were asked to do poster work for the LNER. This is how Anna Zinkeisen saw Dovercourt in 1933.

HUNSTANTON

ILLUSTRATED GUIDE FROM SECRETARY ADVANCEMENT ASSOCIATION
OR ANY L·N·E·R AGENCY.

7. Hunstanton, by Wilton Williams. This delightful design was published in 1929.

THE NIGHT PARADE

HARWICH FOR THE CONTINENT
DAY AND NIGHT SERVICES
THE HOOK–FLUSHING–ANTWERP–ZEEBRUGGE–ESBJERG

8. Frank Mason was among the best marine artists of his time, and he produced this quad royal under the title 'The Night Parade' in 1933. The artist used the same title in a 1935 version of the poster and also a carriage panel in similar style.

9. Tom Purvis produced many eye-catching designs for folders and handbills as well as posters. He came up with this quad royal in 1934 long after he had been accepted as one of the LNER's 'big five' artists.

ROYAL STATION HOTEL

YORK

PART OF THE L·N·E·R HOTELS SERVICE

FOR PARTICULARS OF TARIFFS APPLY RESIDENT MANAGER

10. This double royal poster produced by Arthur Michael in 1935, was one of a series for the Hotels Department. The scene depicted is in the rather splendid ballroom at the Royal Station Hotel, York, during one of their popular dinner dances.

No.6
The Donkey Boy

Travel cheaply by L·N·E·R

11. The reader will know by now that the LNER Advertising Department had a particular liking for posters in sets or series. Following this practice, Frank Newbould was commissioned in 1931 to produce a set of six double royals under the general title of *East Coast Types*. Shown here is number 6, *The Donkey Boy*.

Meet the sun on the East Coast

IT'S QUICKER BY RAIL
ENGLAND'S DRIER SIDE

12. When it came to the preparation for the 1939 holiday season, Cecil Dandridge coined the slogan 'Meet the Sun on the East Coast'. The actual artist is not known, because the work was carried out by Bossfield Studios who actually employed outside artists as and when required. The name Bossfield was actually an amalgam of the names of the proprietors of the studio, messrs Boss and Stanfield.

"WEST RIDING LIMITED"

THE FIRST STREAMLINE TRAIN
BRADFORD LEEDS LONDON
[KING'S CROSS]

MONDAYS TO FRIDAYS
commencing 27th September 1937

BRADFORD dep 11.10 am		**LONDON** dep 7.10 pm	
EXCHANGE		KING'S CROSS	
LEEDS dep 11.31		**LEEDS** arr 9.53	
CENTRAL		CENTRAL	
LONDON arr 2.15 pm		**BRADFORD** arr 10.15	
KING'S CROSS		EXCHANGE	

LONDON & NORTH EASTERN RAILWAY

Opposite: 13. When it came to the launch of the West Riding Limited in 1937, the Advertising Department gave the whole design and print contract to the Baynard Press. Charles Shephard, who was in charge of Baynard's studio, came up with this superb stylized picture of the streamliner. Shephard, who always signed his work 'Shep', carried this design through the whole of the publicity material for this train.

Right: 14. It can be seen from this poster that Frank Newbould's cover for the 1938 *Holiday Handbook* was very much more in keeping with the purpose of the book.

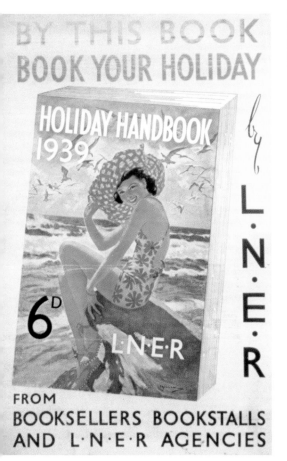

15. A change of artist for the 1939 edition of the *Holiday Handbook* brought this 'glamour' design from Arthur Michael. It may be of interst to know that this particular poster was one of several that were found under the linoleum floor covering of an Aberdeen station where they had lain for nearly fifty years.

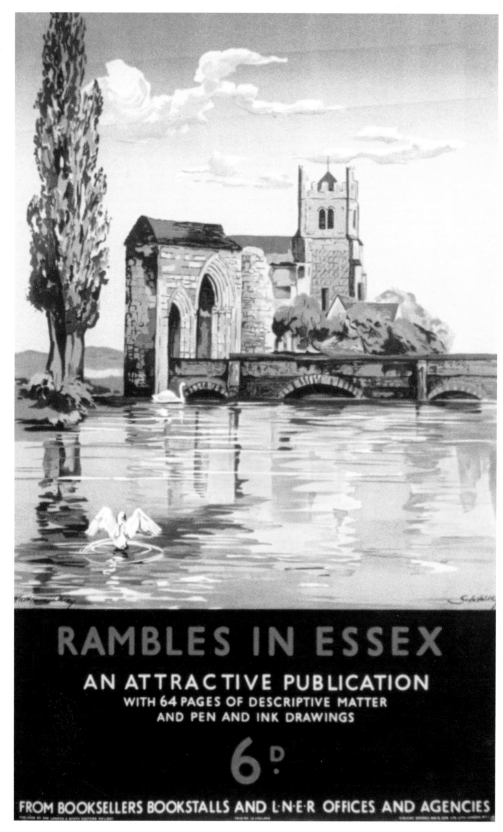

RAMBLES IN ESSEX

AN ATTRACTIVE PUBLICATION
WITH 64 PAGES OF DESCRIPTIVE MATTER
AND PEN AND INK DRAWINGS

6ᴰ

FROM BOOKSELLERS BOOKSTALLS AND L·N·E·R OFFICES AND AGENCIES

16. Many posters were published to advertise the *Rambles* booklets. This double royal is from 1938 and was designed by Shabelsky.

RAMBLES
IN
HERTFORDSHIRE
PRICE SIXPENCE
LONDON AND NORTH EASTERN RAILWAY

**RAMBLES IN NOTTINGHAMSHIRE
AND THE DUKERIES**
PRICE SIXPENCE
LONDON AND NORTH EASTERN RAILWAY

17, 18, 19, 20. Seen here are some more of the popular rambles booklets.

RAMBLES IN ESSEX
PRICE SIXPENCE

LONDON AND NORTH EASTERN RAILWAY

RAMBLES IN NORFOLK
PRICE SIXPENCE

LONDON AND NORTH EASTERN RAILWAY

"EAST ANGLIAN"
LONDON-IPSWICH-NORWICH

"THE CORONATION"
LONDON-EDINBURGH IN 6 HOURS

"THE SILVER JUBILEE"
LONDON-NEWCASTLE IN 4 HOURS

"WEST RIDING LIMITED"
LONDON-LEEDS-BRADFORD

THE FOUR STREAMLINERS
L·N·E·R ACHIEVEMENT
ALL FOR YOUR FURTHER COMFORT

Above: 22. Tom Purvis produced this quad royal in 1938. It appears that the crew of the Silver Jubilee were taking their dog with them.

Opposite: 21. This large *1001 Travel Recipes* folder was published in 1934 and was distributed on a fairly restricted basis by post. It opened out to about the size of a quad royal poster.

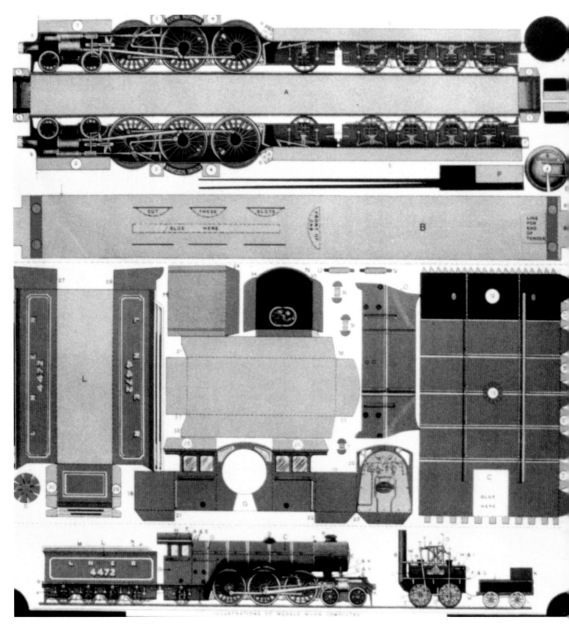

23. Among the items that could be purchased from the LNER's stand at the British Empire Exhibition of 1924 was this cardboard cut-out model of *Flying Scotsman* and *Locomotion*.

The *Varieties* posters were initially used only in the Central London area, but were later also used in Manchester. They were first published in December 1928 and were used up to the beginning of the Second World War. The example shown is believed to be from January 1932.

By the 1940s, the LNER's letterpress posters were being standardised in this format.

The letterpress poster shown is typical of the type in use in the mid-1930s. The colouring and Gill Sans typeface make for easy reading. Curries were official contractors to the LNER.

The Varieties posters were initially to be used in the London area only, mainly being displayed at the underground stations and similar places where it was usual to see theatrical bills. The posters were changed on a weekly basis and were used to give details of excursions and trains to special events, such as race meetings and football matches, etc.

The varieties posters were very successful, and toward the end of 1929, the scheme was tried in Manchester. Dandridge's idea raised a lot of favourable comment in the advertising world and the colourful posters were given a good review in the *Railway Gazette* of January 1929.

The varieties posters were used up to the Second World War, and at one time were even resurrected by British Railways in 1954. During the LNER years there were 1,040 editions published which amounted to some 500,000 posters in total, although very few seem to have survived.

Although the LNER had used the phrase before, it was in early 1933 that a firm decision was taken to 'adopt' the slogan 'It's Quicker By Rail' and use it on all LNER posters where appropriate.

With the outbreak of the Second World War there was a rapid increase in the number of letterpress posters produced. Because of the constantly changing situation at this time, the timetable posters were being reprinted almost on a monthly basis and in order to keep the staff aware of the 'current' timetable, these were printed with various coloured inks to help identify the operative bill.

It was the large number of letterpress posters being produced that prompted Cecil Dandridge to introduce a bolder standardised format early in 1941. The new design incorporated a ¾in blue border at the sides and bottom, and a large 4in border at the head. The heading was completed with the LNER totem.

This standard format was later expanded to the use of different coloured borders for various types of announcement, all of which were described in the company's *Manual of Advertising Practice*.

What must have been the last LNER letterpress poster was in December 1947, and was headed 'Railway Executive, Transport Act 1947'. This was of course the official announcement of nationalisation.

Handbills, Folders and Pamphlets

The LNER were prolific producers of handbills, and in the mid–1930s were turning out some forty million a year. Taking 1930 as a good example, £56,000 was spent on printing handbills alone, the production of which could have been initiated by any of the three advertising offices at London, York or Edinburgh.

The Advertising Department had nearly ninety printing companies who would regularly contract for the work as required and not forgetting the company's own works which also turned out large numbers of handbills.

A look through some of the LNER's handbills will show that one was produced for just about every event that the company could find reason to run a special train. One such bill dated July 1928 advertises a 'Special Half Day Excursion To View An Atlantic Liner (The Cunard SS *Franconia*) At Liverpool'.

The train ran from Leicester, Loughborough, Nottingham and Sheffield. The third class fares ranged from 4s 6d (22½p) to 6s 9d (34p) return. Meals were available in the dining car, luncheon outward and supper on the return could be had for an inclusive charge of 5s (25p).

The conditions of issue of these excursion tickets are of some interest. On the outward journey the passenger was only allowed to take small handbags etc., but

L·N·E·R
SPECIAL
HALF-DAY
EXCURSION
(Dean & Dawson's)

Thursday
12th July

TO VIEW AN
ATLANTIC LINER
(The Cunard S.S. " Franconia ")
AT LIVERPOOL

Also the
GLADSTONE
GRAVING DOCK

This handbill, dated July 1928, was for a special half-day excursion, it will be seen that the trip was actually organised by Dean & Dawson.

on the return, the company was more accommodating in permitting passengers to take up to 60lb of goods, except that 'furniture, linoleum, musical instruments, cycles and mail carts' were not permitted. Quite where one would obtain a 'mail cart' or 'roll of linoleum' whilst viewing the *Franconia* was not stated.

The Advertising Department were always aware of the need to make handbills and pamphlets more attractive. In 1928 the artists Tom Purvis and A.R. Thompson were engaged to design the covers of some of that year's outputs. This incidentally was the first work that Thompson did for the LNER.

Unlike some of the other railway companies, the LNER in the main seemed to prefer the use of white paper with coloured type. One method of making handbills more eye catching, and was used from about 1928, was the use of a coloured diagonal band across one of the top corners of the bill. In fact this treatment was still being used up to the 'Meet The Sun' campaign of 1939.

In 1929 Tom Purvis was again commissioned to design a series of humorous illustrations that were to be used at the head of a set of letterpress posters and their

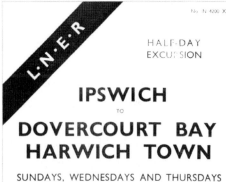

Above: The cover of this 1928 pamphlet was designed by A.R. Thompson. This was the first time that Thompson had worked for the LNER.

Above right: Also of 1928 vintage, this pamphlet cover was designed by Tom Purvis.

Right: It was thought that the diagonal band across the corner of handbills made them more attractive without increasing the cost. This treatment was used for several years – this particular bill is dated April 1934.

WEEK-END TICKETS

between

ANY TWO STATIONS

(including Irish Port Stations)

AT SINGLE FARE AND A THIRD

(Plus fractions of 3d.)

DAY EXCURSION TO

Edinburgh

Whit-Monday 25th May

CUP FINAL

THE STADIUM, WEMBLEY

Saturday, 27th April, 1929

EARLY HOLIDAYS

PERIOD EXCURSIONS
(Holiday Return Tickets)

to the

Lincolnshire &

Midland Counties

WHITSUN HOLIDAYS

DEAN & DAWSONS' DAY EXCURSION TICKETS TO

EDWINSTOWE
and OLLERTON

WHIT-MONDAY, 25th MAY

FROM	TIMES OF DEPARTURE		RETURN FARES. THIRD CLASS.	
			To Edwinstowe.	To Ollerton.
	A.M.	P.M.	s. d.	s. d.
CHESTERFIELD (MARKET PLACE)	10 15	1 10	2 2	2 4
ARKWRIGHT TOWN	10 23	1 18	1 9	1 11
BOLSOVER	10 28	1 23	1 5	1 7
SCARCLIFFE	10 33	1 29	1 2	1 4
SHIREBROOK NORTH FOR LANGWITH	10 46	1 37	0 11	1 1
WARSOP	10 51	1 42	0 7	0 9
EDWINSTOWE ....arr.	10 59	1 48		
OLLERTON ....arr.	11 3	2 49		

Passengers RETURN the SAME DAY ONLY from OLLERTON at 6-54 p.m.
and EDWINSTOWE at 6-58 p.m.

PASSENGERS ARE REQUESTED TO OBTAIN THEIR TICKETS IN ADVANCE.

"WEEK-END" TICKETS

Between any two stations by any train (including Irish Port Stations)
At Single Fare and a Third (plus fractions of 3d.)

OUTWARD BY ANY TRAIN. .... RETURN BY ANY TRAIN.

FRIDAYS, at or after 4-0 a.m........Following SATURDAY, SUNDAY, MONDAY or TUESDAY

SATURDAYS.............................Following SUNDAY, MONDAY or TUESDAY

SUNDAYS................................Same Day or following MONDAY or TUESDAY

Where through fares are not in operation, Week-end Tickets will be issued upon 48 hours notice
being given at the station from which the journey will be commenced.

Minimum Fares :—First Class, 4/0 ; Second Class (where fares in operation), 3/3 ;
Third Class, 2/6.

Week-end Tickets are not issued between Glasgow and Clyde Piers, nor to London Metropolitan,
District or Tube Railway Stations.

FOR FULL PARTICULARS SEE SPECIAL BILLS.

Tickets and bills can be obtained any time in advance at the Company's Booking Offices
and Stations ; also from Dean & Dawson Ltd., 25 Cavendish Street, Chesterfield ; and the
usual Agents.

For further information apply to the District Manager, Lincoln ; or the Passenger Manager,
Liverpool Street Station, London, E.C.2.

London, May, 1931. .... O.T. .... No. 588

For a Programme of Holiday Tours, write to or call at Dean & Dawson's Offices.

2,000 .... FOR CONDITIONS OF ISSUE SEE OVER.

LONDON & NORTH EASTERN RAILWAY

REDCAR RACES.

DEAN & DAWSON'S THROUGH EXCURSIONS TO

REDCAR

WHIT-MONDAY, 25th MAY

FROM	TIMES OF DEPARTURE			RETURN FARES
	A	B	C	
	A.M.	A.M.	A.M.	THIRD CLASS
KIVETON PARK	..	5 0	..	9/6
KIVETON BRIDGE	..	5 4	..	
SHEFFIELD (VICTORIA)	..	..	6 40	
BROUGHTON LANE	..	..	6 45	9/0
TINSLEY	..	5 35	6 50	
ROTHERHAM & MASBORO'	..	5 40	7 0	
ROTHERHAM ROAD	..	..	7 3	
PARKGATE & ALDWARKE	..	..	7 5	
KILNHURST	..	5 55	7 10	8/6
SWINTON	4 50	6 0	7 15	
MEXBORO'	5 0	..	..	
CONISBORO'	5 5	..	..	
BOLTON-ON-DEARNE	..	..	7 25	
FRICKLEY	..	..	7 35	
MOORTHORPE	..	..	7 40	8/0
ACKWORTH	..	..	7 45	
PONTEFRACT	..	..	7 55	7/6
FERRYBRIDGE	..	..	8 0	
REDCAR ....arr	7 48	9 2	10 25	
	E	F	F	

THE "TOTE" WILL BE AT THIS MEETING.

Arrangements have been made with the Sheffield Corporation for Vehicles to meet the
return excursion trains at Sheffield Victoria Station to convey passengers along the various
City Tramway routes. Fare 6d. (Children 3d.)

Car or Bus tickets must be purchased at time of booking at the Booking Office, or from the
Company's Office, 63 Market Place, Dean & Dawson's, 43 Fargate, G. Haywood, 15 Waingate,
and Althams, Ltd., 605 Attercliffe Road, and 10 Dixon Lane.

E—Via Doncaster. .... F—Via Frickley

R.T.

7,000 .... FOR RETURN TIMES, CONDITIONS OF ISSUE, ETC., SEE OVER. .... No. 693

Another attempt to make handbills more attractive was this set of six bills with humorous headings that were designed by Tom Purvis in 1929. These headings were repeated on identical posters.

~Football~

MATCH at TOTTENHAM

TOTTENHAM HOTSPUR

v.

BOLTON WANDERERS

Tuesday, 27th December, 1927

SPECIAL CHEAP

Half-day Football Trip

TO

Northumberland Park

From			At	Return Fare 3rd Class	Returning the same day. At
			p.m.	d.	
Gospel Oak	...	...	1 40	9	
Junction Road	...	...	1 44	8	
Upper Holloway	...	...	1 46	7	
Hornsey Road	...	...	1 48	6	p.m.
Crouch Hill	...	...	1 50	6	4 43
Harringay Park	...	...	1 53	5	
St. Ann's Road	...	...	1 57	5	
South Tottenham	...	...	2 1	3	
Northumberland Pk. arr.			2 5		

Northumberland Park station is close to Park Lane entrance to the ground.

In the event of the Match being postponed, the Special trains will be cancelled and the Cheap tickets will not be issued.

Children under 3 years ... age. free. 3 and under 12, half-price. No luggage allowed, excepting small handbags, luncheon baskets, or other small articles intended for the passenger's personal use during the day. The tickets are not transferable and will only be available on the date, by the trains, and at the stations named. Issued on any other date by any other train, or at any other station than those named, the tickets will be forfeited, and the full ordinary fare charged. No allowance made for any ticket lost, mislaid or not used. The Company give notice that tickets for this Excursion are issued at a reduced rate, and only on condition that the Company shall not be liable for any loss, damage, injury or delay to Passengers arising from any cause.

London 18th., 1927.

LNER

13579 11 rt- 5000   No. 4031

PRINTED AT THE COMPANY'S WORKS STRATFORD

For a few years cheap trips to football and rugby matches were advertised on standardised handbills such as this.

duplicate handbills. Purvis was asked to produce sketches with particular events in mind, such as football matches, race meetings etc. One particular amusing design shows an office desk with telephone ringing, and the young office secretary hand in hand with her boss, both carrying weekend cases and beating a hasty retreat from the office. This sketch was used to advertise the 'Week End Tickets' handbill.

Around the late 1920s the Advertising Department produced a standardised football excursion handbill. This was provided with a heavy wavy line as a border having the LNER totem at the bottom and the word Football as a heading. The bills were printed in this 'skeleton' form and issued to contract printers as required, to print on the details of the particular train and match.

This practice seems to have lasted some three or four years and was dropped, probably because it was found cheaper to give the local printer a block of the LNER totem and have just one run of print, rather than go through two separate printers.

The printers of this May 1930 pamphlet were among the first to use the LNER's new typeface, although it must be said that only the cover was set in Gill Sans.

When handbills were used to advertise any trains with fares at less than the normal rates, the company was obliged to print the rather lengthy 'conditions of issue' of the ticket, some of which have already been referred to. These conditions took up a considerable amount of space on the handbill, which often meant it had to be printed on both sides, with a consequent increase in printing costs.

Sometime in the mid-1930s, Dandridge took this matter up with the company solicitor who, after some deliberation, agreed that most of the conditions could be omitted from the handbills, subject to the full conditions being shown on the current timetables, and a note to this effect put on the handbill.

Sometimes the Commercial Advertising Department were able to sell the space on the back of handbills. One such successful occasion was in 1932, when the backs of one million handbills were sold to Messrs Hobson, Trimble & Co. to amplify the benefits of their particular brand of corn plasters.

From around 1933, LNER handbills and pamphlets took on a more attractive appearance, with increasing use being made of the Gill Sans typeface.

Not wishing to lose the LNER's business, it was obvious that the contract printers were under some pressure to equip themselves with the new typeface.

A considerable number of the pamphlets produced in the late 1930s, have artwork covers in some form and many are still a pleasure to see. It is unfortunate that in many instances the work is unsigned and one can but make a guess at the artist. However some of them were given barely discernible initials and present-day researchers may look for Frank Newbould whose work was sometimes initialled FN or just N, likewise Tom Purvis would use TP. A.R. Thompson's first pamphlet cover was initialled with a T, and John Bee used a large block capital B.

With the improvements in photographic techniques in the 1930s, some rather nice photogravure folders were produced to advertise three of the facilities that had been pioneered by the LNER. These were Camping Coaches, Weekly Holiday Season Tickets and Week End Cruises. These folders were very well designed and easy to use, and must have sold many additional tickets for these services.

The LNER's efforts to encourage the pursuit of rambling far exceeded that of any of the other main line railway companies. This eleven-page pamphlet of 1940 was full of details, including train fares, times and various routes. It also included a full-page advert for the seventeen Rambles booklets then available. The attractive cover design was by John Bee.

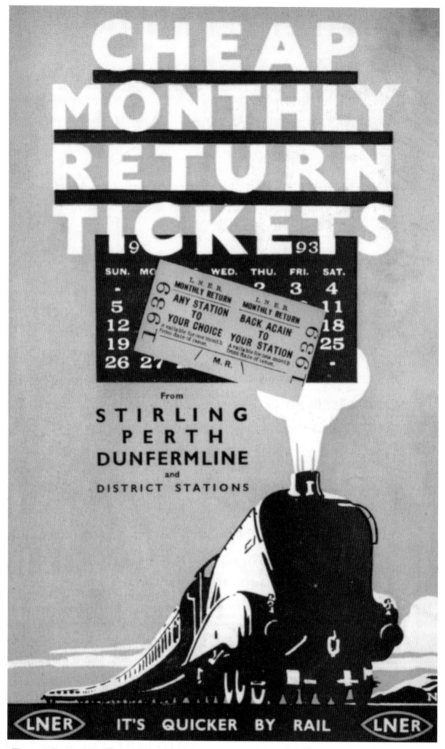

The excellent cover design of this 1939 pamphlet is by Frank Newbould.

Left: Another 1940 pamphlet design by John Bee, which was among the last to be published for several years due to the Second World War.

Right: The 1936 season of the Eastern Belle saw the publication of this pamphlet, the artist unfortunately unknown.

Left: There were programmes of Sunday Half-Day Excursions from the London termini. This is for April 1937 with cover by Frank Newbould.

Right: The LNER had many printers who would tender for work. This printing was done by Love & Malcolmson of Redhill, Surrey.

CHEAP HOLIDAY TRAVEL FACILITIES

EASTER 1 9 3 8

Including Train Services from
KING'S CROSS
LIVERPOOL ST.
MARYLEBONE
and
SUBURBAN STATIONS

CHEAP MONTHLY RETURN TICKETS pages 2 to 20
NIGHT TRAVEL TICKETS pages 21 to 25
SPECIAL ADDITIONAL TRAINS,
Good Friday, 15th, Easter Monday, 18th,
Tuesday, 19th April, page 19

LNER

Left: Much was made of the main companies' one penny per mile third class tickets. This is one of the LNER's 1937 'bargain offers'.

Right: Another attempt to add interest. The photograph was posed – in 1936 it was *de rigueur* to have a cigarette at the bar.

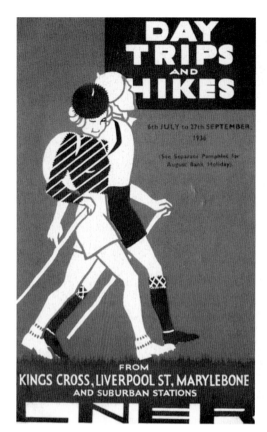

Left: Simple but very eye catching. Unfortunately the artist is unknown for this 1936-1937 rambling pamphlet.

Right: The LNER initiated 'Week End Cruises' in 1932. The folder for the 1937 programme is shown with an excellent picture of the LNER's RMS *Vienna* by Frank Mason.

Right: The 1939 folder for the 'Week End Cruise' programme was photographic throughout, but RMS *Vienna* is still front page.

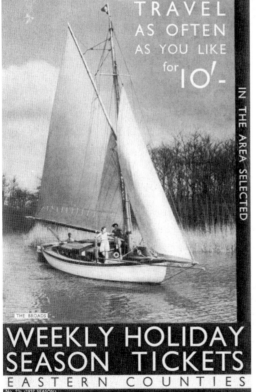

Left: Another innovation was 'Weekly Holiday Season Tickets', around 1933. Tickets were available for some thirty-five areas in England and Scotland.

Left: Another folder for 'Weekly Holiday Season Tickets' – this time the 1939 season.

Right: The LNER did on occasion publish material specifically for foreign tourists. The pamphlet shown was one such example. It was for distribution in the United States, where the company had a permanent representative. The date of the publication is thought to be late 1920s, and the cover is by Austin Cooper.

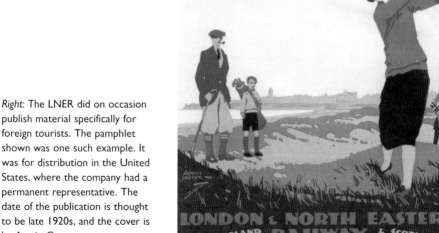

LMS & L·N·E·R

RAILWAY
GRAIN SACKS

are in short supply, unfortunately without any prospect of the situation improving

With every desire on the part of the Railways to help farmers, merchants and other users, demands for sacks can only be met by keeping the number ordered to the minimum and by a strict observance of the railway regulations governing the hiring, transfer and return of sacks

HIRING—Supplies of sacks should not be drawn earlier than actually required nor in excess of the number that can be filled immediately

TRANSFERS—A transfer of sacks with grain between farmer and merchant and between merchants is permitted provided the transferrer gives to the railway company in writing, within 7 days, full particulars of

such transfer: this permission does not however release the original hirer from his liabilities

RETURN — Railway sacks should be returned without delay: they should not be held for storage nor for any other purpose

ACCOUNTS — Prompt settlement of accounts is essential in view of present-day staff difficulties

HELP US
TO HELP YOU

September, 1942

Printed in Great Britain by Knapp, Drewett & Sons Ltd., London and Kingston-on-Thames.—23425R.

One of the rather obscure services that the railway companies used to offer farmers was the hire of sacks. This joint LMS-LNER handbill was published by the LNER. The use of two colours at this particular period of severe austerity is something of a surprise.

1934 saw the publication of a superb full-coloured folder, which gave details of all of the LNER holiday literature that was available that year. The folder was entitled *1001 Travel Recipes*, and was said to have been mainly distributed by post to selected addresses in London and the provinces. The folder had a tear-off coupon to make application for the publications, but when fully opened the folder opened to quad royal size, and there is good reason to believe that some were actually used as posters. *1001 Travel Recipes* was an excellent piece of publicity material, but unfortunately seems only to have been published on this one year.

With the outbreak of war the production of most publicity material came to a halt but a few handbills were produced which were for information purposes only. After the war the austerity conditions precluded travel advertising for several years and it was to be well into nationalisation before handbills were seen in any great numbers.

Left: The initials on the suitcase shown on the cover of this 1938 pamphlet give a clue to the artist who was, of course, Frank Newbould. He has also been careful to show two of the circular luggage labels that he designed for the LNER.

Below: Here the *1001 Travel Recipes* has been opened to show a complete list of all the LNER holiday publications available for that year. Also provided was a tear-off slip to obtain any required literature.

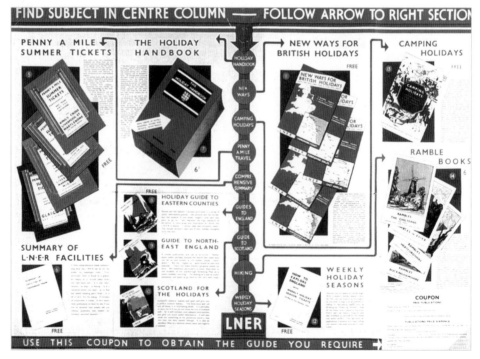

Press Advertising

The LNER was no exception from the other main line companies in spending the greater part of its advertising budget on press advertising, some 40% of its total outlay being spent in this manner.

Most of the press advertisements fell into two categories, the first being announcements of special trains or excursions at reduced fares, and for which newspaper advertisements were found to be particularly effective.

The second type of advertisement was prestige or reminder advertisements, which were a little more general in nature. For this type of advertisement extensive use was made of the higher-class newspapers and magazines, such as the *Times*, *Illustrated London News* and *Country Life,* etc.

The very first press advertisement published by the company was placed in most of the national newspapers during the first week of the LNER's formation in January 1923. It announced the new name of the company and stated the company's aim TO SERVE YOU.

Looking through some of the press advertisements of the earlier years of the LNER, it is easy to see how the larger part of the company's advertising budget

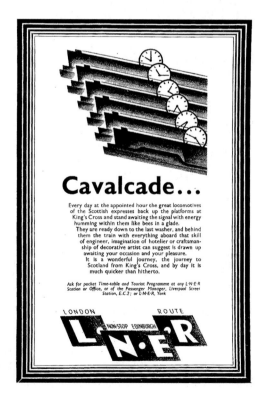

The LNER's Advertising Department referred to this type of press advertisement as a 'prestige' or 'reminder' advertisement. The date is 1932 and the writer seems to have a rather romantic vision of Kings Cross in steam days.

Above: In 1932 the LNER were making much out of the fact that the Flying Scotsman was running non-stop between Kings Cross and Edinburgh.

Right: The Key to Healthy Holidays. From the *Radio Times* of 1930.

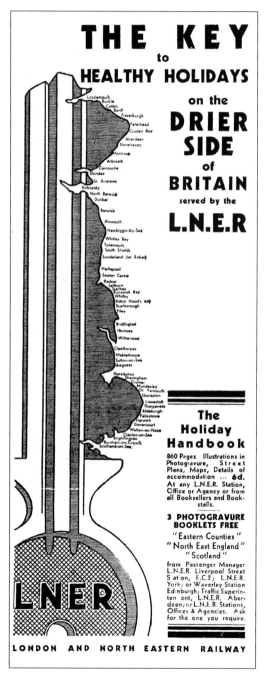

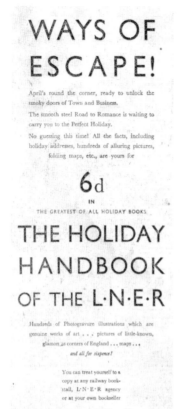

This double column advertisement appeared in the *Daily Express* in March 1929. It has some significance in terms of LNER publicity as it was the very first use of the LNER's new Gill Sans typeface and it was also the first advertisement for the then new *Holiday Handbook*.

This is a 1936 joint press advertisement placed by the LNER. The artwork was by Robert Bartlett.

Another joint advertisement placed in the national press in 1939.

was used. Nine and ten inch double columns in *The Times* were never a cheap proposition, also bearing in mind that many of these advertisements incorporated art work of some form which added to the cost.

One may be led to think that there was also the cost of employing a poet in some instances. The phraseology and claims made in some advertisements seemed to more than stretch the imagination. A 10in double column taken in the *Times* for 16 June 1927, extols the virtue of the 'Glorious Yorkshire Coast' and asks, 'Do you desire the gaiety and movement of the holiday throng, sauntering on spacious promenades and among elaborate flower gardens, while the ear is soothed with the music of the waves? These and all the resources of a modern resort are provided by Scarborough, the queen of watering places'.

This advertisement, like most of the East Coast publicity, contained a comment to its being 'on the drier side'. This slogan was used by the LNER for many years and was a reference to the fact that rainfall records indicated that the eastern side of the country had a significantly lower rainfall than the western.

When the first edition of the *Holiday Handbook* was published in 1929, the Advertising Department was also preparing to use the new Gill Sans typeface, and it was thought that some early trials should be carried out in some press advertisements. A 10in double column was taken in the *Daily Express* for Tuesday 19 March of that year and the bold advertisement read 'Ways of Escape, The Holiday Handbook of the LNER'.

The first joint railway press advertisements were placed in the national newspapers in November and December 1928. It had been agreed that each company would take a turn at producing the advertisement. These first advertisements were placed by the LMS for the Christmas and New Year's train services. For the following Easter it was the LNER's turn and they commissioned Montague Black to produce quite a striking little picture depicting four locomotives with the slogan Easter, Faster, Easier, Cheaper in the smoke trail of the locomotives.

Reginald Mayes, who was the Chief Staff Artist for the LMS, has related that it was always thought so important in all of these joint advertisements and posters to get the company initials in the correct alphabetical order.

In the early years of the LNER they were always referred to as the L and NER, and were therefore entitled to be placed before the LMS. However, at some time in the mid-1930s it was noticed that they were using an ampersand (the abbreviated form of 'and') between the L&N and that they ought therefore to be placed after the LMS. A look at advertisements after this date will reveal that the LNER were moved back one place. No doubt those at Euston Road got some measure of satisfaction from this event.

It was often the case that the artwork from a pictorial poster or booklet cover could be adapted for use in a press advertisement. As well as some possible saving in costs, this gave a continuity to the advertisement. A very good example of this was Frank Newbould's series of 'East Coast Types', which were originally designed as double royal posters. Newbould was paid an additional fee of £31 10s (£31.50) to adapt these, and with additional text they appeared in many newspapers and magazines in 1931.

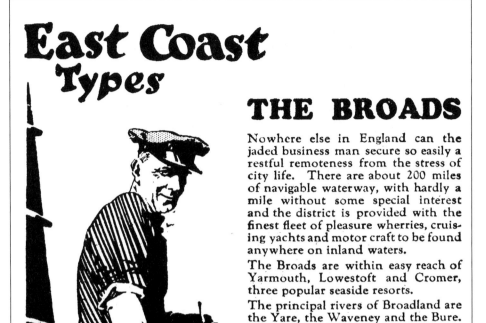

East Coast Types

THE BROADS

Nowhere else in England can the jaded business man secure so easily a restful remoteness from the stress of city life. There are about 200 miles of navigable waterway, with hardly a mile without some special interest and the district is provided with the finest fleet of pleasure wherries, cruising yachts and motor craft to be found anywhere on inland waters.

The Broads are within easy reach of Yarmouth, Lowestoft and Cromer, three popular seaside resorts.

The principal rivers of Broadland are the Yare, the Waveney and the Bure. There are about fifty Broads, the larger of which have a water area of from 200 to 400 acres. Chief yachting centres — Wroxham and Oulton Broads.

No. 1
The Broads
Wherryman

FREE BOOK "**EASTERN COUNTIES**" from L N E R Stations, Offices and Agencies, or from Passenger Manager, L N E R, Liverpool Street Stn., E.C.2; York, or Waverley Stn., Edinburgh, or Traffic Supt., L N E R, Aberdeen.

Full particulars of boating arrangements, yachts for hire, &c., may be obtained from the Norfolk Broads Bureau, Broadland House, 22, Newgate Street, London, E.C.1 (Guide 300 pages, price 6d. post free).

TRAVEL CHEAPLY BY L·N·E·R

Frank Newbould was paid an additional fee to modify his *East Coast Types* poster designs for use as press advertisements. This was no.1, *The Broads Wherryman*, from the *Radio Times* of 1931.

This double royal poster was part of the big joint advertising campaign of 1936. The artwork was used in both press and poster publicity.

The mid-1930s saw the railway companies beginning to realise that they could well lose much of their freight traffic to the road hauliers. A big joint effort was called for, and the LNER's part in this was to call Frank Newbould in again to produce a series of designs that could be used on posters as well as press advertisements. Newbould's excellent work, coupled with some good text, would make it difficult to believe that it could be improved upon today.

The freight campaign was quickly followed by the railways call for a 'square deal' for which no less than 136 national and provincial newspapers were used. As we have seen, this had to be set aside for the LNER's 1939 'Meet The Sun On The East Coast' holiday season.

'Is Your Journey Really Necessary' became one of the most popular slogans of the Second World War. The slogan was coined by Bert Thomas, who uses it here in a national press advertisement of 1943.

September 1939 saw the outbreak of the Second World War, from which time the press advertisements took on a completely different approach. Several of the LNER's contributions to the wartime press advertisements were illustrated by Bert Thomas, and it was his designs that carried the caption 'Is Your Journey Really Necessary'.

It was well into nationalisation before the railways managed to get away from press notices and start to advertise once again.

Chapter Five

THE FAMOUS TRAINS AND LOCOMOTIVES

No history of LNER publicity would be complete without mention of some of the named trains and locomotives.

Whilst each of the other main line companies had their famous named trains and locomotives, none achieved the long lasting fame of such trains as *The Flying Scotsman*, *Silver Jubilee* and *Coronation*.

In his article 'Advertising the LNER', published in the last edition of the *LNER Magazine*, A.J. White summed it up when he said: 'Named trains are always good prestige subjects and were exploited to the full. The Flying Scotsman was our standby until the advent of The Silver Jubilee and The Coronation, and then the LNER was really made famous throughout the world!'.

The Flying Scotsman

The name 'Flying Scotsman' is almost synonymous with that of the LNER. The company called it 'the world's most famous train', a title that not many would argue with. The name had been unofficially given to the train which, for many years prior to the grouping, had left Kings Cross at ten o'clock every weekday morning, bound for Edinburgh. However on the formation of the LNER in 1923 it was agreed that the name should be officially adopted.

It was also in 1923 that one of Nigel Gresley's new Pacific locomotives was brought into service with the number 1472. Within a year the locomotive had been named *Flying Scotsman*, and at the same time the locomotive was re-numbered 4472, a number that was to become almost as well known as the name.

It is probably true to say that during the company's twenty-five-year existence, nothing generated more publicity than the name 'Flying Scotsman'. The locomotive was put on display at the British Empire Exhibition of 1924 and 1925 where it aroused a great deal of attention. It was said that the locomotive was put on display in order to associate her with the now officially-named express train to Scotland.

Prior to 1928 it had been essential that on its journey to Scotland, the Flying Scotsman made certain stops to change crews and take on water. From 28 May of that year, the Flying Scotsman began running the 393 miles to Edinburgh without stopping.

This non-stop journey was a world record for a regular scheduled service, although because of a longstanding agreement with the LMS, the overall journey time had to remain something over eight hours.

Having mentioned the LMS, it must be said that they got wind of the LNER's intention to commence the non-stop running and, trying to be 'one up', they arranged just three days before to run their Royal Scot in two small parts which just enabled them to reach Scotland non-stop. However this arrangement proved somewhat impractical and could not be maintained on a regular basis.

The Flying Scotsman's non-stop runs were made possible by the special loco-motive tender that had been designed by Gresley and which had a small corridor through which the train crews were able to change over whilst still travelling.

The LNER were given some fine publicity out of the press coverage given to the first non-stop run. Crowds of people were at Kings Cross to see the train away, and nearly half of the back page of the *Daily Express* for the following day was given over to a fine photograph of the train leaving the London terminus.

Shortly after commencing the non-stop runs and purely as a publicity stunt, arrangements were made with Imperial Airways for a party of journalists to be flown to Scotland by the well-known Capt. Gordon Olley, while a similar group from the press were to be carried north by the Flying Scotsman.

The idea was that the train and aircraft would rendezvous over the Royal Border Bridge at Berwick, where photographs were to be taken, and radio messages were to be sent from the aircraft to the train. The aircraft was then to carry on, with the intention of having its passengers at Waverley Station to meet the train.

As it happened, in his overconfidence of the aircraft's greater speed, Olley deviated from his course several times to point out particular points of interest.

In his book *A Million Miles in The Air*, Olley jokingly admits he rendezvoused with the wrong train. It appeared he had not travelled quite so fast as he had antic-ipated and the train he saw was the *Junior Scotsman* which ran some minutes behind the main train. He related that after realising his mistake, he opened the throttles, eventually sighting the right train. After making radio contact, Olley flew on to Edinburgh, but unfortunately the train had beaten him to it by a few minutes.

During its lifetime the Flying Scotsman was provided with a cocktail bar (one of its specialities was a Flying Scotsman cocktail) a buffet car, restaurant cars, ladies retiring room and a hairdressing saloon.

Another innovation was the provision of a cinema coach where the films were compiled exclusively for the train by Pathé Gazette. It should however be noted that a cinema coach had first been tried on the Flying Scotsman as far back as March 1924, when it ran from Kings Cross with a selected audience of journalists.

By special arrangement with W.H. Smith & Son and John Menzies, newspapers and periodicals were sold on the train. Special notepaper and envelopes could also be purchased at 4d (1½p) per packet. The LNER booklet *On Either Side* was also available from the attendant.

As another publicity stunt, portable radios were installed in the restaurant car on 1 June 1938, so that passengers could receive the results of the Derby. It was also in 1938 that two completely new trains were constructed for the service. As ever, the company were looking for some good publicity out of the launch of the new train, and with this in mind a demonstration run was arranged for 30 June.

The press and many invited guests were taken from Kings Cross to Stevenage, in some rather ancient Great Northern coaches. They were hauled by the old Stirling Locomotive No.1, which had been removed from the LNER Museum at York and, in the strictest secrecy, specially renovated for the occasion.

On arrival at Stevenage, the passengers were de-trained for a photographic session, and were then taken on to Grantham in the luxury of the new air-conditioned train.

As with many things, the commencement of the Second World War brought an end to all the ballyhoo, but not the Flying Scotsman. The train ran throughout the war and into nationalisation, but unfortunately was never to regain the glory of the 1920s and 1930s.

The Silver Jubilee

It was the advent of Nigel Gresley's magnificent streamlined locomotives in 1935, and the luxurious trains they made possible, that gave the LNER one of its best ever publicity opportunities.

The company had of course many named trains prior to the introduction of the 'streamliners', but none (with the possible exception of the Flying Scotsman) caught the public imagination as much as the launch of the Silver Jubilee in September 1935.

The Silver Jubilee booklet was given to each passenger on the train as a souvenir of their journey. The booklet did contain a lot of useful information such as train times, connecting services, seat plans, etc.

The name was bestowed on the train in honour of King George V celebrating twenty-five years on the throne. In the greatest secrecy, four superbly-designed locomotives had been built. The first one, *Silver Link*, being delivered for running-in trials on 13 September.

On Friday 27th of that month, Britain's first streamline train gave a demonstration run for the press and invited guests. It was on this trip that the train twice reached just over 112mph, a world record at that time.

The Silver Jubilee service was run between Newcastle and London. Leaving Newcastle at 10.00 a.m., and arriving at Kings Cross at 2.00 p.m. The train was then prepared for its return journey, which departed Kings Cross at 5.30 p.m., and arrived at Newcastle at 9.30 p.m.

The train was originally made up of seven coaches, but because of demand this was later increased to eight. There was a supplementary charge for the service, which was 5*s* (25p) for first class and 3*s* (15p) for 3rd class.

The Advertising Department gave top priority to publicising the new train, most impressive of which was the superb poster by Frank Newbould. The slogan 'Britain's First Streamline Train' appeared on all the publicity material, including the press advertisements and the special booklet given to every passenger.

Prior to the launch of the new train, the LNER management had been quite unsure of the passengers' reaction to being charged a supplementary fee for the high-speed service. A hint of this was given in the foreword of the booklet given to each passenger. This said, '*The Silver Jubilee* will occupy an exceptional share of the running lines and must be well loaded if it is to pay its way. The retentionof the train as a permanent feature of the timetable will depend upon its popularity!'

All doubts were soon dispelled however, for the train was always in great demand. In fact it was noted that in a little over two years, the supplementary fares alone had paid for the building of the train.

The Silver Jubilee ran very successfully up to the Second World War, when it was put into storage. At the end of the war the coaches were dispersed and used on some minor services, after which most were scrapped in the 1960s.

The Coronation

Encouraged by the success of the Silver Jubilee the LNER management needed little persuasion to embark on further development of the streamline services, and it was on 5 July 1937 that the Coronation entered service. The train was named *Coronation* by permission of King George VI, to celebrate his Coronation year.

Reginald Mayes was actually the Chief Staff Artist for the LMS. He produced this original artwork sketch for a joint LMS-LNER double royal poster in 1938.

Special silverware was designed for the streamline Coronation service in 1937. it was provided with this new LNER monogram.

Five more streamlined locomotives had been built to haul the new train, each one being named after a country of the British Empire. The locomotives were, *Dominion of Canada, Commonwealth of Australia, Dominion of New Zealand, Union of South Africa* and *Empire of India.* The locomotives were described as being similar to the Silver Link Class and were finished in Garter Blue with stainless steel trim and lettering.

The train itself was made up of nine specially-constructed coaches, the last of which was said to be scientifically streamlined into a 'beaver tail'. This last coach was to be used as an observation car for the use of which one was charged an additional supplementary fee of 1*s* (5p) per hour, special tickets being printed for this purpose. The Coronation was to run on the East Coast route between Kings Cross and Edinburgh, and was timed to complete the 393-mile run in six hours. During a special pre-launch run on 30 June 1937, the train, in the charge of *Dominion of Canada,* touched 109mph on the return run to London.

The train had been designed with silent running in mind, and to this purpose it even had specially-designed cutlery, with flat handles that would not rattle. The cutlery was also inscribed with a new LNER monogram.

Special crockery was also provided and, like the china on the other high speed services, was to give the company something of a headache with the high rate of breakages. This was to come to a head in early 1939, when the dinning car attendants were asked to make a special note where these were thought to have been caused by the high speeds.

A souvenir booklet was also provided for passengers on the Coronation. Again the cover design was by Frank Newbould.

Coming back to the actual day of the first public service, it was reported that excitement had been growing during the day, and by the timed departure of 4.00 p.m., there was an estimated crowd of 2,000 on the platform at Kings Cross. The news of the first run had spread far and wide, and crowds turned up to see the train through all the stations on the route.

The length of the run made it necessary to have two trains, in order to provide a service in both directions. It was said that the departure from Edinburgh had been carried out with just as much excitement.

As in the case of the Silver Jubilee, a supplementary charge was made which for the Coronation was 6s (30p) first class and 4s (20p) for third class for the whole journey, or slightly less if one travelled only to the intermediate stops of York on the down run or Newcastle on the up journey. Also like the Silver Jubilee, a souvenir booklet giving full details of the train and journey was given to every passenger.

The Coronation again proved that the LNER had struck the right note, and the train ran very successfully up to the Second World War, when it was placed in safe storage at Ballater in Aberdeenshire. After the war the train was refurbished at Doncaster in 1948, but was soon dispersed into other services.

The West Riding Limited

The third of the streamlined trains went into service on 27 September 1937, with the name The West Riding Limited. The train was to run between Bradford, Leeds and London, and was timed to run the 186 miles at an average speed of 68mph.

The train was actually timed to leave Bradford at 11.10 a.m., with arrival at Kings Cross at 2.15 p.m., whilst the down service left London at 7.10 p.m., arriving in Bradford at 10.15 p.m.

Two A4 Class streamlined locomotives were allocated to run the Leeds–London service, and these were named *Golden Fleece* and *Flying Shuttle*. These locomotives had been so named to emphasise the close association of the service with the woollen industry which was mainly located in the West Riding of Yorkshire.

The two 'streamliners' could not be used on the Bradford–Leeds section, because of some severe gradients, and it was left to two powerful tank locomotives to run this part of the route.

The new carriages of the train, which were almost identical to the Coronation set, were superbly fitted out, and the external colour scheme was Marlborough Blue above the waist and Garter Blue below. As before, a souvenir booklet was given to each passenger.

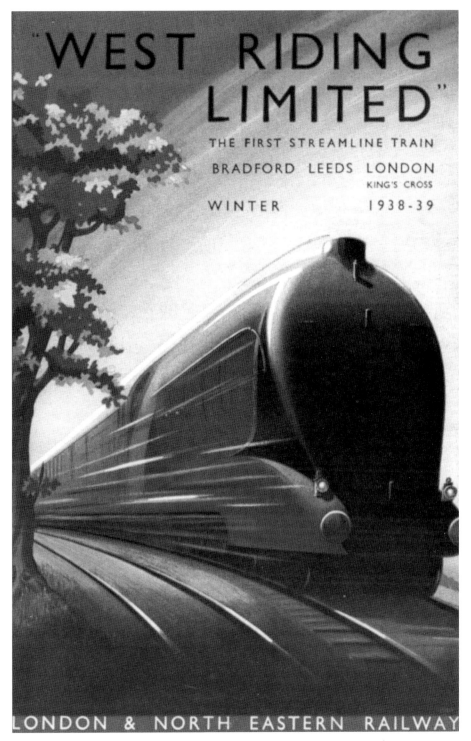

The souvenir booklet for the West Riding Limited was very similar in content to the previous booklet, but the cover design was Charles Shephard's stylized A4 design.

Like the other streamline trains, the West Riding coaches were put into store for the duration of the war, but were not restored to their former service until 1949. At this time six of the coaches were among the first to be painted in the new British Railways crimson and cream livery. For a time these were used on the new West Riding service, but were eventually replaced by standard British Railways stock.

The East Anglian

The East Anglian was the name bestowed upon a new service run between Norwich and London (Liverpool Street), with one intermediate stop at Ipswich.

The train was made up of six specially-constructed coaches which were fitted out to the highest standards, and like the other streamline services, had armchair seating. However, the external finish to the coaches was of standard LNER teak panelling. This it was thought was partly to play down the high speed image that was so desirable with the other streamline services.

Although the new train marked a distinct advance in the service between Norwich and London, it was not possible to reach the high speeds being achieved by the streamliners out of Kings Cross. One reason for this was the fact that the two locomotives scheduled to take the service were two B17 'Sandringham' class locomotives that had been specially dressed up with a streamlined casing. One could perhaps say 'sheep' in 'wolves' clothing.

The two locomotives had originally been named *Tottenham Hotspur* and *Norwich City* but, with the provision of the new streamlined casing, they were renamed *East Anglian* and *City of London* respectively. As a matter of fact their former names were handed on to two other B17s.

On Monday 27 September 1937, the day of the inaugural run, it was said that the station platform at Norwich was crowded with enthusiastic well-wishers who wanted to see the start of this new LNER venture.

The service, which like the other streamliners was only run on weekdays, was timed to depart Norwich at 11.55 a.m. with arrival in London at 2.10 p.m. The return service left Liverpool Street at 6.40 p.m. and arrived at Norwich at 8.55 p.m. It was decided that as the East Anglian would not achieve the speed of the fully-fledged streamliners, the company could not justify a ticket surcharge.

Although the East Anglian was withdrawn during the war, the coaches did continue in service. After the war the train was restored in its original format, but the coaches were replaced with standard BR stock in the 1950s. As a matter of interest the two locomotives had their streamlined casings removed in 1951.

It is thought that there were no pictorial posters printed for the East Anglian, but this excellent quad royal letterpress was printed at the LNER printing works in 1938.

The Northern Belle

The evening of Friday 16 June 1933 saw the launch of yet another LNER 'first'. This was the inaugural run of the first railway cruise train, which the company had named the Northern Belle.

It was a specially fitted out train that was to leave Kings Cross on Friday evenings during the month of June. It was to go on a week-long tour of the Border Country and Scotland.

The idea had been put forward by the Chief General Manager, who in January 1933 asked the Passenger Managers' Committee to work out details for a season of trial runs that year. He had in mind the ever-increasing competition from some of the coach companies who had started running seven-day coach tours.

These coach tours were similar to the 'land cruises' that the Great Western Railway had been running for some years, in that each night was spent at an hotel. In the case of the Northern Belle, however, each passenger was provided with a first class sleeping compartment as well as a reserved seat in the restaurant car.

The 'cruises' were strictly limited to sixty passengers, and the whole trip was organised on the lines of an ocean cruise. The special luggage labels included a space for the passengers 'cabin' number and the train crew did not refer to the front and back of the train but to the 'fore' and 'aft'.

The Northern Belle cruise train was another LNER innovation when it was launched in 1933. This is a press advertisement of 1938.

The train was made up of fourteen coaches, which could be divided into a day portion comprising two staff coaches, a kitchen car, two first class restaurant cars and two coaches used for a hairdressing salon, ladies retiring room, general retiring room, writing and smoking rooms. The night portion was made up of six first class sleeping cars, two of which had shower baths, and a luggage car.

Many of the company's senior officers were at Kings Cross to see the first 'cruise' away on the evening of the inaugural run. Sir Ralph Wedgwood was ill and could not attend, but he sent a telegram to the Station Master with the following message: 'Please convey to the passengers and crew of the Northern Belle my best wishes for a successful first cruise. Regret I cannot be there to wish good luck in person'.

Over the years the itinerary was to vary slightly, but most nights would be spent with the train standing in sidings while the passengers slept. During the day, the night portion of the train would sometimes be left, whilst the day portion did a particular tour. Both portions would be reunited for the next overnight stop.

Some meals were arranged at hotels and there were motor coach and steamer trips all included. One particular highlight of the cruise was a stop for a few moments on Glenfinnan Viaduct, where the passengers enjoyed the magnificent views down Loch Shiel.

Most of the national newspapers of the day were invited to send a reporter on the first cruise, and upon their return their accounts of the trip were without exception, full of praise for the new venture.

For the first 'season' of cruises, each passenger was presented with a souvenir handbook, a stationery case and a set of bridge playing cards, as a memento of the cruise. In subsequent years, the passengers were given just the souvenir booklet which for, the Silver Jubilee year of 1935, was a special silver edition tied with a 'jubilee blue' bow.

The fares for the Northern Belle cruises remained at £20 per person and, with a full complement of passengers, which was always the case, the company made around £300 profit per cruise.

There was no doubting the popularity of the Northern Belle. It was said that for every 'sailing', the platform at Kings Cross was packed with well-wishers. The cruises ran every year up to 1939, and like most of the LNER's other special services were brought to an abrupt halt by the war.

Mallard and the World Speed Record

What must have been one of the greatest achievements of the 'streamliners', was the setting of the all-time world speed record for steam locomotives. This was accomplished on 3 July 1938 when A4 locomotive No. 4468 *Mallard*, together with six of the Coronation coaches and a dynamometer coach, were taken on what was announced as tests of a new braking system. There was, however, a rumour circulating among those in the know, that Gresley was after the speed record held by the LMS at 114mph.

The intention was to run the train from Wood Green to Grantham and return, and it was recorded that the outward journey was taken very easy. After turning the engine at Grantham, the run back to London was commenced by steady acceleration of the train.

By the time some six miles had passed the speed had reached 116mph and with speed still increasing, the train went through Little Bytham at 120mph. For just a few seconds a maximum speed of 126mph was attained which was a record for steam engines that has never been beaten.

In achieving this speed, one of *Mallard*'s big ends had 'run' its bearing, and the locomotive had to call it a day at Peterborough. *Mallard* was taken back to Doncaster Works where within a few days the bearing had been repaired and the locomotive was returned to service.

From the publicity point of view, the LNER never made much out of gaining the world record. Even when pushed by the press, the comments were very low key. The following day's *Daily Telegraph* published a very small picture of *Mallard*, over which was the heading 'British train speed record 125mph attained on test run.'

Strangely, it would seem that the company never produced any advertising material based on *Mallard*, not even an official postcard. It is, however, nice to see that the locomotive that put the LNER on top of the world has at least been preserved for future generations to see.

The Hush Hush Locomotive No.10000

Towards the end of 1929, it was strongly rumoured that the LNER was building something new in locomotive design. For some weeks the Press Section had been under pressure from the newspaper world to give some information as to what all the secrecy was about.

It was on 10 December 1929 that the 'covers' were taken off *Locomotive 10000*, an express engine of revolutionary design. The locomotive had been designed by Nigel Gresley not so much for more power or speed, but in order to achieve greater fuel economy.

The locomotive was built with a high-pressure marine-type boiler, which because of its size, could not be provided with a conventional chimney. In anticipation of running non stop from London to Edinburgh, it had been fitted with a corridor tender to allow a change of crew without stopping.

When it was running, *No.10000* was principally used on the York-Edinburgh service, although on occasion it did work the Non Stop Flying Scotsman, where it proved to be both powerful and fast.

No.10000 was very often put on show at the LNER open days and rolling stock exhibitions, where a considerable amount of publicity was gained by exploiting its unorthodox design. However *No.10000* was unable to live up to its expectations when in service, the fuel consumption being far greater than had been hoped. Serious problems also became apparent with the maintenance of the engine and it was withdrawn from service on 21 August 1935.

The engine languished at Darlington Works until September 1936, when it was sent to Doncaster Works to be rebuilt with a conventional boiler and streamline casing. It did however retain its original 4-6-4 wheel arrangement and number.

This is one of a set of four official postcards of Locomotive 10000.

In its rebuilt form *No. 10000* did some magnificent work throughout the Second World War, hauling some exceptional loads, but was eventually scrapped shortly after nationalisation.

Cock o' The North

May 1934 saw the completion of another unorthodox Gresley locomotive from Doncaster Works. This was the 2-8-2 P2 Class locomotive No. 2001, to be named *Cock o' The North*.

It was built for the Edinburgh–Aberdeen service, and at the time was the most powerful express locomotive in Great Britain. After a short period undergoing trials, it was sent to Kings Cross to work the London–Yorkshire Expresses, but after a matter of weeks, was moved north to Scotland.

In December 1934 a second P2 engine was completed, being numbered 2002, and given the name *Earl Marischal*. This locomotive was similar to 2001, but with some detail differences. Later in 1936 four similar locomotives were constructed. However, these were semi-streamlined with wedge-shaped front ends.

During 1937, 2001 and 2002 were rebuilt to match the four later locomotives in the series, but it was in its original form that *Cock o' The North* was most publicised. It was repeatedly put on show at the company's exhibitions and open days, becoming a great favourite with the public.

In 1942, and to the complete disgust of all Gresley worshippers, all six of the P2s were, it was felt unnecessarily, rebuilt by Edward Thompson who, on the death of Gresley, had been given the job of Chief Mechanical Engineer.

Chapter Six

MISCELLANEOUS PUBLICITY (1)

The LNER Magazine

Following the amalgamation in 1923, it was in some respects a considerable time before the company became a single cohesive unit. One very good instance of this was the fact that from its formation in 1923 until December 1926, two staff journals were still being published under the names of the *Great Eastern* and *North Eastern and Scottish* magazines.

After four years it was obvious that the company should be provided with one 'all line' staff magazine. The proposal came from Sir Ralph Wedgwood (who had been knighted in late 1923). In the Chief General Manager's Circular, dated 6 December 1926, he said, 'The London and North Eastern Railway Magazine will be the name of the new publication, which will replace the existing *Great Eastern* and *North Eastern and Scottish* Magazines. The first edition will appear on 7th January, the price being 2*d* [1p] per copy. The magazine will form a record of the many activities of the staff and their organisations'.

It was obvious that the Chief General Manager was anxious to see the company working more as a single unit. His circular went on to say 'The new venture has the fullest support and good wishes of the directors and officers of the company, and I shall personally take the keenest interest in its progress'.

The previous magazines were both first published in 1911 and their volumes were identically numbered. It was decided to carry on with this sequence, making the first issue of the new magazine volume 17. Like one of its predecessors, the new magazine was to be printed at the company's printing works at Stratford Market.

The heyday of the *LNER Magazine* was undoubtedly the mid to late 1930s, when on average each copy ran to some sixty to seventy pages. Compare this with

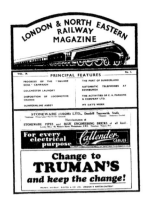

The face of the LNER Magazine changed over the years.

the depths of the Second World War when about twenty pages was the best that could be achieved.

Some 45,000 copies of the first issue of the magazine were sold, and this can be compared with the sale of 23,000 copies of the last edition. This huge drop in circulation was in the main due to the large reduction in the number of staff that had taken place, particularly during the Second World War.

The last issue of the magazine carried a series of brief reviews from some of the heads of departments. We have already heard of A.J. White's review of the Advertising Department. Another of the reviews was by Cecil Dandridge, and he covered the Passenger Department. His article, entitled 'Progress in Passenger Services' was written in Dandridge's rather succinct style and was of course to be his last in the magazine.

We have seen that it took four years for the LNER to produce one 'all line' magazine, no such time lapse occurred on nationalisation. January 1948 saw the appearance of the first *British Railways Magazine* Volume 1 No.1, there was however a small note in brackets '(successor to the *LNER Magazine*).'

Lantern Slides and Films

It is difficult to say exactly when the LNER first loaned out their lantern slide lectures, but these were made available to colleges, schools and club secretaries, etc. and were loaned free of charge.

The idea behind the slide shows, which were in the main about the tourist areas served by the company, was the hope that after seeing these places on the screen, clubs, groups or even individuals, would arrange their outings there.

In 1929 there were sixteen sets of slides available, each set having its printed lecture notes that would be read out to the audience. An additional set was added in 1930, and by 1934 there were twenty sets available.

1939 saw a total of twenty-three sets of slides being available, these covered such diverse places as Southend-on-Sea, Edinburgh and the Lowlands, and the North East Coast. There were even five sets dealing with Holland, Belgium, Northern Italy, Germany, and Switzerland, showing of course that you got there via Harwich and the LNER Shipping Services.

Two sets of slides were really for the railway enthusiast, and these were the 'Centenary of Railways', and the 'Railway Museum, York'. Applications to obtain the Lantern Slides was made to The Advertising Manager in London or Edinburgh.

A 1939 advertisement for the loan of LNER lantern slides.

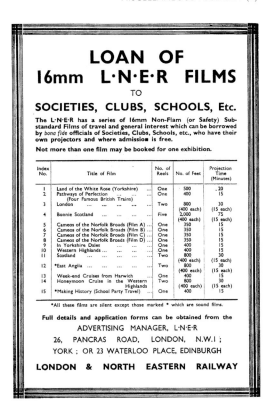

In 1935 the LNER began to loan out 16mm films. This is a 1939 press advertisement for the service.

The LNER slide shows were very popular; it was noted that in 1929, no less than 1,500 sets were sent out on loan. It was the popularity of the slide shows and the general improvement in cinematography, that led the company into its first loan of 16mm films in late 1935.

Again the films were only available to clubs and similar organisations. There were certain stipulations in borrowing the films, these were that only one film could be booked for one show, no charge could be made for admission to the show, and you had to have your own projection facilities. At one time there was also a requirement that there had to be a minimum audience of not less than fifty persons.

By 1939 there were fifteen films available, all except two of which were silent. As with the slides, the films in the main were on places to be visited, by LNER of course. However, one film was about school party travel, and another had the title 'Pathways of Perfection', which was a joint film about a famous train from each of the main line companies.

Following the declaration of the Second World War, and the evacuation of schoolchildren from some of the large towns, a note in the *LNER Magazine* said: 'some LNER lantern slides and films were providing welcome entertainment for evacuated children in rural districts that were situated far from amusements to which the children were accustomed'. It must have been shortly after this note was printed, that all so-called scenic lantern slides and films were withdrawn for security reasons.

Over the years a certain amount of almost free publicity was obtained in co-operating with filmmakers in the production of several commercially-produced films. One of the earlier productions in this respect was in 1930, and was in the very early days of sound films. The title of the film was *The Flying Scotsman*. Seeing that the company were likely to get a great deal of publicity out of the film, they gave all the assistance possible.

The production of *The Flying Scotsman* was by British International Pictures, who were given exclusive use of the Flying Scotsman for six weeks, with runs being made from Kings Cross to Edinburgh. A great deal of the film was also shot on the LNER's Hertford Loop line, with the line being taken over on several Sunday mornings.

In 1935 a short newsreel film was actually made of the publicity trip by an Imperial Airways aircraft and the Flying Scotsman en route to Edinburgh (see Chapter 5). The film shows the radio being used between the aircraft and the train, and there were air to air and air to ground shots taken from an accompanying aircraft.

The LNER terminus at Marylebone was always a popular location among film producers whenever station scenes were required. Another well used location in 1935 was Waverley Station, Edinburgh, together with the Forth Bridge, which was extensively featured in the original version of *The Thirty-nine Steps*.

Whenever it became known that a cinema was showing a film featuring the LNER, the Advertising Department would arrange with the cinema management to provide some free publicity at the local station, in exchange for a display of LNER publicity material in the cinema foyer.

Much was made of showing films onboard trains, but the LNER were well in the lead when as early as 1924 W.M. Teasdale arranged with a film company to give some demonstration film shows in an adapted first class kitchen car attached to the Flying Scotsman.

In May 1935, a passenger brake van was converted to a 'cinema coach', which was used on the service between Kings Cross and Leeds. Following the success of this, a further 'cinema coach' conversion was carried out in 1936 for use on some Leeds to Edinburgh trains. A charge of 1s (5p) was made to see the show, which lasted about one hour. These popular 'cinema coaches' ran up to the Second World War, when they were withdrawn and converted back to their original use.

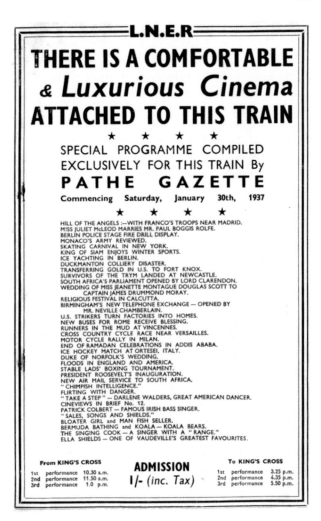

1935 also saw the LNER showing films on one of their scheduled train services. This handbill gives the early 1937 programme.

Text within the handbill image:

L.N.E.R

THERE IS A COMFORTABLE
& *Luxurious* *Cinema*
ATTACHED TO THIS TRAIN

★ ★ ★ ★

SPECIAL PROGRAMME COMPILED
EXCLUSIVELY FOR THIS TRAIN By
P A T H E G A Z E T T E
Commencing Saturday, January 30th, 1937

★ ★ ★ ★

HILL OF THE ANGELS :—WITH FRANCO'S TROOPS NEAR MADRID.
MISS JULIET McLEOD MARRIES MR. PAUL BOGGIS ROLFE.
BERLIN POLICE STAGE FIRE DRILL DISPLAY.
MONACO'S ARMY REVIEWED.
SKATING CARNIVAL IN NEW YORK.
KING OF SIAM ENJOYS WINTER SPORTS.
ICE YACHTING IN BERLIN.
DUCKMANTON COLLIERY DISASTER.
TRANSFERRING GOLD IN U.S. TO FORT KNOX.
SURVIVORS OF THE TRYM LANDED AT NEWCASTLE.
SOUTH AFRICA'S PARLIAMENT OPENED BY LORD CLARENDON.
WEDDING OF MISS JEANETTE MONTAGUE DOUGLAS SCOTT TO
        CAPTAIN JAMES DRUMMOND MORAY.
RELIGIOUS FESTIVAL IN CALCUTTA.
BIRMINGHAM'S NEW TELEPHONE EXCHANGE — OPENED BY
        MR. NEVILLE CHAMBERLAIN.
U.S. STRIKERS TURN FACTORIES INTO HOMES.
NEW BUSES FOR ROME RECEIVE BLESSING.
RUNNERS IN THE MUD AT VINCENNES.
CROSS COUNTRY CYCLE RACE NEAR VERSAILLES.
MOTOR CYCLE RALLY IN MILAN.
END OF RAMADAN CELEBRATIONS IN ADDIS ABABA.
ICE HOCKEY MATCH AT ORTESEI, ITALY.
DUKE OF NORFOLK'S WEDDING.
FLOODS IN ENGLAND AND AMERICA.
STABLE LADS' BOXING TOURNAMENT.
PRESIDENT ROOSEVELT'S INAUGURATION.
NEW AIR MAIL SERVICE TO SOUTH AFRICA.
" CHIMPISH INTELLIGENCE."
FLIRTING WITH DANGER.
" TAKE A STEP " — DARLENE WALDERS, GREAT AMERICAN DANCER.
CINEVIEWS IN BRIEF No. 12.
PATRICK COLBERT — FAMOUS IRISH BASS SINGER.
" SALES, SONGS AND SHIELDS."
BLOATER GIRL and MAN FISH SELLER.
BERMUDA BATHING and KOALA — KOALA BEARS.
THE SINGING COOK — A SINGER WITH A " RANGE."
ELLA SHIELDS — ONE OF VAUDEVILLE'S GREATEST FAVOURITES.

From KING'S CROSS	ADMISSION	To KING'S CROSS
1st performance 10.30 a.m.	**1/- (inc. Tax)**	1st performance 3.25 p.m.
2nd performance 11.50 a.m.		2nd performance 4.35 p.m.
3rd performance 1.0 p.m.		3rd performance 5.50 p.m.

Best-Kept Stations

Five months after the formation of the company in 1923, the Chief General Manager issued a circular advising that the directors had decided to extend the scheme of awarding prizes for the 'best-kept station'. The prizes were to be as follows: A special prize of £10 each, to the three best station gardens in each section; a first class prize of £7 10s (£7.50); a second class prize of £5 and a third class prize of £3.

The 'class' prizes were to be awarded on a points basis, and it is of interest to see how these were to be allocated.

General condition of the station	Maximum 8 points
Tidiness of platforms and lines	Maximum 7 points
Cleanliness and smartness of staff	Maximum 5 points
Conditions of water closets	Maximum 5 points
Condition of waiting rooms and offices	Maximum 5 points
Neatness of notices, timetables and advertisements	Maximum 5 points
Cleanliness of lamps and windows	Maximum 5 points
Cultivation of flowers and shrubs	Maximum 60 points
Total	100 points

It is easy to see from the allocation of points that the main object of the competition was to get the staff interested in growing plants and shrubs at the stations. That this objective was achieved can be judged from the fact that in 1927 there were sixty-five special and first class prizes awarded. By 1939 this number had risen to 150.

It was left entirely up to the individual station master to decide if they wished to enter the competition, and the station master of any prize-winning station was required to distribute a proportion of the prize money to members of the staff who assisted with the work.

A lot of the work carried out by staff on their gardens was done in their own time, often just for the pride that they gained from seeing the results of their labours.

During one year it was reported that the stationmaster and porter signalman at Inverbervie, had moved over three tons of pebbles from the local beach to lay out a design in the form of the LNER totem on the bank behind the station platform.

In later years some of the garden designs were getting quite sophisticated. In 1938 the staff at Greenlaw Station, near Berwick, were recorded as having constructed a magnificent flowerbed with a floral clock as a centrepiece. The clock was 7ft in diameter and was worked by a system of batteries. A pendulum arrangement was located under the signal box which sent a regulated pulse to the clock, which it was said kept perfect time.

By 1936 some of the local station gardens were becoming so well known, that it was decided to run an excursion to view them. The train ran from Newcastle to Kelso stopping at six selected stations en-route. The excursion was so successful that three more trains were run that year. Not to miss out on this, the Advertising Department at York got word of the special trains, and arranged to leave a supply of current advertising material at each of the stations to be visited.

Like many things, the Best-Kept Station scheme was more or less brought to a halt by the Second World War. One reason for this was that the increasing shortage of food meant that everybody was being urged to 'dig for victory' and any spare garden space was soon turned over to growing vegetables.

Many of the LNER's prize-winning stations of pre-1939 are sadly no more, and just as many of those that are left retain little if any of their former glory. Over the years the hard work and dedication of the station staff won a great deal of admiration and affection for the company.

The LNER Aircraft Purchase Scheme

During the Second World War, and more for patriotic reasons than publicity, many large companies, county councils and similar organisations took part in what was known as the 'aircraft purchase scheme'.

For their part, the LNER were quick off the mark, starting in August 1940. The idea behind the scheme was that employees would make small donations of cash which were collected by the company and forwarded to the Ministry of Aircraft Production. When a sufficient amount of cash had been donated, an aircraft would then be purchased under the name of the contributing company or organisation.

NOTICE TO THE STAFF

One of the greatest needs of the moment to help us beat the enemy is the supply of more and more Bomber and Fighter Aircraft. In this we can all help, and our assistance can be given in practical form with a definitely personal touch

What better way can there be than by contributing directly towards the cost of aircraft to bear the name of the London & North Eastern Railway? A scheme, of which full particulars are being circulated, has been arranged to enable the whole of the staff of the L.N.E.R. to participate in this way, and I sincerely hope that it will meet with a wide and immediate response

C. H. NEWTON,
Chief General Manager

August, 1940

This is the notice to staff that initiated the LNER's Second World War aircraft purchase scheme. Aircraft spotters will notice that the aircraft shown is a Bristol Blenheim.

APRIL, 1941.

A Real 'Flying Scotsman'

All grades and staff of the L.N.E.R. have added to the splendid work which they are doing in the national effort, by subscribing to their own Spitfire fund, by the result of which two new machines have been added to the strength of the R.A.F. One plane bears the appropriate name of "Flying Scotsman" and we hope that it will succeed to become as famous as its namesake on rails. The second machine will be named "West Riding."

The new airplane "Flying Scotsman" and subscribed for by the staff of L.N.E.R.

Correspondence.

To the Editor, 'RAILWAYS.'

Dear Sir,

May I point out that one or two remarks on signalling in Mr. Coles's interesting Belgian article in the March issue are not quite accurate? Distant signals are not painted *exactly* similar to the British equivalent, but have arrow headed ends, instead of fishtailed ones, with the black V mark pointing outwards. I was well acquainted with the man who completely reformed the Belgian signalling before the last war and again after it, Monsieur L. P. A. Weissenbruch, the Secretary of the International Railway Congress Association for many years. When he decided to introduce the yellow distant signal in place of the older square red disc, together with the British type bracket signals for junctions, the fishtailed arm was in use for another purpose, so his distant arms had to take another shape. Up to then, junction signals had been mounted vertically one above each other, and the arm relating to the high speed route was fishtailed to enable it to be recognised from among the others. These pre-war (1914) signals were two position upper quadrants and the signalling was thus very like our present standard British type. After the war, when so much damage had been done, Monsieur Weissenbruch decided to adopt the three position principle, which is not difficult to apply to mechanical signals worked by double wires, but he abandoned splitting distant signals. In place of this he used a three-position distant and the standard indications are :

HOME SIGNALS :—
Horizontal, RED light—Stop.
45 degrees, YELLOW light—Caution, next signal is at Stop.
90 degrees, GREEN light—Proceed.

DISTANT SIGNALS :—
Horizontal, YELLOW light—Caution, next signal is at Stop.
45 degrees, YELLOW light and GREEN light—Attention, reduced speed at next signal.
90 degrees, GREEN light—Proceed.

The 45 degree position of the distant arm is used either to show that a diverging route is signalled at the junction

The intention of the LNER scheme was to purchase a Bristol Blenheim but, with much more glamour attached to the newer fighter aircraft, the company actually went on to purchase Spitfires. On reading the magazine, one would get the impression that only two aircraft were purchased. In a short article in the February 1942 edition, some news was given about the LNER's Spitfires. It was said that the first aircraft, named *Flying Scotsman* of course, 'was doing a grand job and was still going strong', and some news of its activities would be given at a later date.

The second aircraft had been named *West Riding*, and the magazine explained that this Spitfire had unfortunately been shot down whilst escorting our bombers on a raid, but luckily the pilot had 'baled out'. The next and final mention of the aircraft was in the September 1942 magazine, which went on to relate that *Flying Scotsman* had completed many operational trips with great success!

It seemed curious that no further mention of the Spitfires was ever made in the wartime issues of the magazine, but from a study of RAF records, one is able to shed a little more light on this apparent mystery.

It appears that there were in fact four Spitfires purchased under the name of the LNER. The first two were *West Riding* (No.R7274), of whose fate we have heard, and *Flying Scotsman* (No.X4913). It is recorded that X4913 was taken on charge (received by the RAF) on 3 January 1941. After a short spell with the RCAF it went to 53 Operational Training Unit on 22 July 1941.

On 3 November 1941 X4913 was taken up on a routine training flight from which it never returned. It was not until some seven months later that the wreck of the aircraft was found near the summit of Pen-Y-Fan in the Brecon Beacons where presumably in low cloud it had flown into the top of the mountain.

The next LNER Spitfire (X4914) was named *Cock o' The North* and must have been purchased at the same time as *Flying Scotsman*, as the numbers were consecutive. It was actually taken on charge by the RAF one day before X4913.

After moving to various squadrons, it was received by No.58 Operational Training Unit where, on 17 June 1943, it was taken up on a routine training flight. It appears that whilst doing some unauthorised aerobatics with another aircraft, the two planes collided in mid-air with the result that the pilot of *Cock o' The North* was killed and the aircraft was a total loss.

The last of the LNER Spitfires (BM202) was again named *Flying Scotsman*, and was taken on charge on 13 March 1942. It seems to have moved between two or three squadrons but little seems to be known of its ultimate fate, except that it appears to have survived the war, being struck off charge (written off) on 21 June 1947.

In view of the untimely and seemingly unnecessary destruction of the first *Flying Scotsman* and *Cock o' The North*, it is of little surprise that no more information was ever published in the magazine. In those hard days during the Second World War, it would have been a bitter pill to swallow for the LNER staff, to have heard what happened to the aircraft purchased by their hard-earned collections.

Chapter Seven

MISCELLANEOUS PUBLICITY (2)

Exhibitions

The first and almost certainly the largest exhibition that the LNER ever partici-
pated in was the British Empire Exhibition held at Wembley in 1924 and 1925.
The company had a large stand on which it displayed George Stephenson's
Locomotion which was the first steam locomotive to haul a passenger train in 1825.

Locomotion had originally been built for the Stockton & Darlington Railway Co.
which in 1863 had been absorbed into the North Eastern Railway, and it was
therefore truthfully said that the LNER's locomotives could trace direct genealog-
ical descent from Stephenson's old masterpiece.

Displayed next to *Locomotion* was the LNER's pride and joy, *Flying Scotsman*, and
between them these two locomotives were said to have attracted thousands of
visitors to the LNER stand.

The LNER had something more of an involvement with the exhibition than
just taking stand space. A large part of the land on which the exhibition was built
had been owned by the company, and they no doubt came to some agreeable
terms with the organisers over its use.

The LNER also took what they thought was something of a gamble when they
constructed a new branch line with a station giving direct access to the exhibition.
The station was named 'Wembley Exhibition', and many thousands of visitors
were to use it over the two-year period.

A considerable amount of the construction materials were delivered to the site
by the LNER, not the least of which was a 1,000-ton load of sand from the beach
at Mablethorpe in Lincolnshire, which was used to construct a 'treasure island' at
the 1925 event.

L·N·E·R

British Empire Exhibition,
WEMBLEY, 1924.

ADDITIONAL FACILITIES

Commencing MONDAY, 16 JUNE, 1924,
and on WEEK-DAYS until further notice,

CHEAP RETURN TICKETS
will be issued to

WEMBLEY

EXHIBITION STATION
(L.N.E.R.)
and

WEMBLEY PARK (Met. Rly.)

by any train due to leave the
issuing stations at or after 9.30 a.m.

AVAILABLE FOR RETURN THE SAME DAY BY ANY TRAIN.

For particulars of fares, routes, &c., see pages 2, 3 & 4.

☞ Passengers are requested to state at the time of
booking to which station they require their tickets.

Right: Thousands of handbills were printed for travel to the British Empire Exhibition of 1924/1925. This one is dated June 1924.

L·N·E·R

British
Empire Exhibition

NON-STOP
TRAIN SERVICE
IN 12 MINUTES

Marylebone
&
Exhibition Station

*(The only Station inside
the Exhibition Grounds)*

23rd April to 5th July inclusive

Left: The British Empire Exhbition was extremely successful and generated a lot of traffic for the LNER. This small timetable folder of April 1924 shows that at peak times there were no more less than eight trains an hour between Marylebone and the LNER station within the grounds.

1925 saw the centenary of the first steam-hauled passenger train, and it was to mark this occasion that the LNER took on the considerable task of organising a large 'Centenary of Railways' event, which took place at Darlington.

The celebrations were officially declared open by HRH the Duke and Duchess of York, on 1 July 1925. The major event however was to be held the following day and was a grand procession of locomotives and rolling stock.

The procession, which was over six miles long, ran between Stockton and Darlington and was made up of locomotives and rolling stock from all four main line companies.

Among the LNER exhibits were the new carriages for *the Flying Scotsman*, while *Locomotion* had been especially withdrawn from the British Empire Exhibition and was hauling a set of replica Stockton & Darlington coaches.

Among the publicity material produced for the 'Centenary', were two pictorial posters, one by Fred Taylor showing *Locomotion* being driven by George Stephenson. The other poster was a head and shoulders portrait of Stephenson, by Andrew Johnson.

This double royal of George Stephenson was by Andrew Johnson and was one of only two pictorials published by the LNER for the Railway Centenary of 1925.

After a busy time with the British Empire Exhibitions and the Centenary cele-brations, a quieter period ensued. 1927 saw the Advertising Exhibition at Olympia, London, one of the first events where the LNER was represented jointly with the other main line companies. The stand was headed 'British Railways' and was really just a public relations exercise to show what the railways were doing for the nation.

During 1929, a large exhibition was held to revive some of the industries in the North East of England, which were beginning to suffer the effects of the trade depression. The 'North East Coast Exhibition', as it was called, was located in Newcastle, and ran throughout the summer.

The LNER made its presence felt by taking a stand in the 'Palace of Engineering'. Among other things on the stand, the company were showing off one of its new Sentinel Cammell rail cars, with which it had high hopes of breathing new life into some of its flagging branch lines.

As well as the stand at the exhibition, the company took one of the pavilions in the grounds. This was used as a general enquiry office, where during a special *Flying Scotsman* week, two of the drivers of the famous train were in attendance to answer any questions. It was said that they boosted sales of the *Flying Scotsman* paperweight to a new all time high.

One of the more popular events organised directly by the railway companies has always been the 'rolling stock' or 'railway exhibition'. 1928 saw the LNER holding ten such shows all of which, to read the reports, were very well attended.

It was usual to make a small charge for admission to these exhibitions, with the proceeds going to a charity. The LNER's management was always prepared to give every assistance to the local organising committees, particularly in ensuring that interesting exhibits were made available.

Of course *Flying Scotsman* was usually top of the bill at local Railway Exhibitions but for two or three years, *Locomotive 10000* was beginning to take pride of place. With its lack of operational success, *Locomotive 10000* was superseded by *Cock o' The North*, but with the advent of the A4 streamliners, *Cock o' The North* and the other P2s tended to take second place.

There were always other attractions at these exhibitions. A favourite that would be frowned on today was to get the 45-ton breakdown crane to hoist an open wagon full of visitors up to a height of 25ft or so, and then to rotate it in the fashion of a roundabout.

An event that took much of the Advertising Department's attention in 1938 was the Empire Exhibition held at Bellahouston Park, Glasgow. The exhibition generated a lot of business both for the LMS and LNER in transporting a large proportion of the exhibits and later the visitors.

The Empire Exhibition ran from May until October, and the railway companies once again combined to take a large joint stand. Each of the four main line companies placed a section of a coach from one of its famous trains on display, that from the LNER being from the 'Coronation' set.

By the close of the exhibition in October, the LNER's share of advertising had amounted to 26,500 posters, 150,000 folders, 50,000 booklets and 1,600,000 handbills as well as a considerable number of press advertisements.

A practice carried on from pre grouping days was the provision of a company office at the major agricultural shows. The office took the form of a small timber shed or tented structure and which in the early days was a fairly rudimentary affair. It would be provided with a desk or two and a few chairs. It was then left to the Advertising Department to provide the external fascia and generally make the whole thing look presentable by judicious use of current advertising material such as posters etc.

In later years it was found more cost effective to attend these shows on a joint basis under the name of British Railways.

Co-operative Publicity

Something that the Advertising Department actively encouraged were the approaches made to them by many of the larger department stores for the loan of publicity material to use as a background for window displays. This would more often occur at Christmas or summer holiday time when the stores were displaying their new season's wares.

Always on the lookout for cheap or even free publicity, the Advertising Department would quite happily provide current pictorial posters, handbills, luggage labels etc. Requests would often be received for such things as porter's barrows, uniforms and even the odd milk churn or two, which all gave a touch of realism to a holiday display and which from the company's point of view kept their name to the fore.

A great deal of free publicity came from companies wishing to jump on the LNER 'bandwagon' by using one of their famous train or locomotive names to publicise their products. The most popular name in this respect was of course *Flying Scotsman* which appeared on many products including biscuit and toffee tins and many unofficial jigsaw puzzles and childrens games.

At one period, a very well known watch manufacturer was advertising its products by stating that Mr Ben Glasgow, driver of the famous *Flying Scotsman*, says 'time is of vital importance in railway working'. The advertisement was complete

This Flying Scotsman jigsaw puzzle was manufactured by Lumar Ltd. The original artwork was by Frank Mason who was commisssioned by the LNER in 1931 to produce a design for a quad royal poster with the title *East Coast Route*. The design was also used on a LNER publicity folder, before Lumar were allowed to have use of the design for their jigsaw puzzle.

The makers of Service Watches used the Flying Scotsman. This advertisement appeared in many periodicals in the mid-1930s – this one was from the *Radio Times* of June 1935.

SAVE 2 WAYS

THE YORKSHIRE PENNY BANK LIMITED

The scheme will apply at the undermentioned branches, where further information may be obtained on application.

BARNARD CASTLE	KIRBYMOORSIDE	RIPON
BEDALE	KNARESBOROUGH	
BEVERLEY	LEYBURN	SALTBURN
BILLINGHAM	LOFTUS	SCARBOROUGH
BISHOP AUCKLAND		SKINNINGROVE
BRIDLINGTON	MALTON	SOUTH BANK
	MARSKE-BY-THE-SEA	SELBY
DARLINGTON	MIDDLESBROUGH	SPENNYMOOR
DRIFFIELD	.. (Linthorpe)	STOCKTON
FERRYHILL	NORTHALLERTON	
FILEY	NORTON-ON-TEES	THIRSK
		THORNABY
GRANGETOWN	PATELEY BRIDGE	
GREAT AYTON	PICKERING	WEST HARTLEPOOL
GUISBOROUGH	POCKLINGTON	WETHERBY
		WHITBY
HELMSLEY	REDCAR	
HOWDEN	RICHMOND	YARM

Travel Vouchers will be accepted at L.N.E.R. Booking Offices at any of these places.

FOR HOLIDAYS

November 1928 saw the Yorkshire Penny Bank enter into a joint venture with the LNER. This advertisement is of 1931 vintage.

with a photograph of Mr Glasgow and a silhouette of *Flying Scotsman*. These, it said, were 'courtesy of the LNER'!

The introduction of the streamlined A4s also encouraged some companies to cash in on the LNER's success. At one time the advertisements for Bear Brand hosiery were saying that their stockings and Silver Link were 'the smartest things in transport'.

Shortly before Christmas 1936, Messrs Gamages (a famous London department store) asked the Advertising Department if they could have on loan some carriage doors, platform trucks, uniforms, posters etc. These were to enable them to design their Father Christmas show around the Silver Jubilee. Especially recorded sounds of the train departing Kings Cross, were to be played, and Gamages confidently expected over 100,000 children and adults would 'travel in the train' with Father Christmas.

It was in November 1928, that a scheme was entered into with the Yorkshire Penny Bank, that was to be known as the 'Thrift and Travel Scheme'. The idea was that one could open what would be called a 'travel account' with the bank, by making deposits of any amount. These deposits received normal bank interest, but if the depositor wished to travel by rail, he or she would obtain a voucher from the bank, which was then exchanged at the booking office for a rail ticket. The cost of the ticket, less 5% discount, was then deducted from the account.

This scheme had certain advantages to the LNER, other than the obvious one of attracting another passenger. Part of the agreement with the bank was that at each of its branches, and initially there were some forty-three of these, there was to be a supply of current LNER literature on display.

In 1931 similar arrangements were entered into with the South Shields Saving Bank and the Savings Bank of Newcastle. These arrangements effectively gave the LNER a major outlet for its publicity material in the high streets of nearly all of the larger towns in the North East of England.

Just before the commencement of the Second World War in 1939, the Eagle Star Insurance Co. co-operated with the LNER's 'Meet the Sun' campaign, by offering 10% reduction in insurance premiums against rained-off holidays when taken on the 'drier side'.

Many of the LNER's staff did their bit to help the company, not least of whom were the Carter's. Any local carnival was always an invitation to them to enter their beautifully turned out horse and carts, which were always decorated with the LNER's current pictorial holiday posters. It all helped to keep the name of the LNER in front of the public.

Enquiry Offices

The LNER inherited numerous enquiry offices from its pre-grouping ancestors, the majority of which were at the larger stations and termini.

Although the enquiry offices did not come under the control of the Advertising Manager, it was his department's responsibility to ensure that their appearance was satisfactory and that the display and advertising material was up to date.

The enquiry offices actually were part of the Passenger Managers Department and were a major outlet for the company's advertising material. In 1929 it was reported that at one of the London offices, no less than 180,000 items of advertising literature had been handed out and that did not include handbills.

The LNER opened a number of new enquiry offices that were not actually located at stations. This was particularly the case in London, where at one time or another they occupied some quite prestigious addresses, in such places as Regent Street, Oxford Street, Piccadilly, James Street and Victoria Street.

The company also had a number of offices abroad, the oldest probably being in New York and which together with it's General Agent H.J. Ketcham, had served the Great Eastern Railway for many years prior to the amalgamation. The New

York office was in fact closed down in January 1934, when a joint venture with the LMS and Southern Railways opened a new office on Fifth Avenue, under the heading of Associated British Railways.

At the same time as the New York office was opened, another joint office was opened in Paris, this time with the involvement of the Great Western Railway as well. As it happened the Paris premises had previously been occupied by the LMS.

A great deal of LNER publicity material was handed out from the enquiry offices on board the Cunard Liners *Queen Mary* and *Queen Elizabeth*, but it must be said that both of these offices were jointly run under British Railways.

There were several advantages in having offices abroad, one of course being that you always advised that the best places to visit were those served by the LNER. Another advantage was that with the LNER's Continental Shipping Services and excellent chain of hotels, it was able to offer a complete tourist service.

The Second World War soon closed most, if not all of the foreign enquiry offices and those at home saw a rapid run down in publicity material. There was, however, a great upsurge of railway passengers during the war period and in this respect the enquiry offices were kept busier than ever with train service enquiries.

The LNER Railway Museum

To the LNER must go the credit for opening the first museum dedicated solely to railway transport, although the basis of the museum had been formed in the days of the North Eastern Railway.

It was an employee of the North Eastern, by the name of J.B. Harper, who first put forward the idea of a railway museum. From the late 1800s he had spent much of his spare time gathering together numerous items of historic railway interest. This collection was stored with the blessing of the North Eastern's management, in the basement of their headquarters offices at York.

It was at a meeting on 29 March 1922 that the powers that be on the North Eastern, gave permission for Harper's collection to be given a more permanent home. The larger items were located in what had been the old repair shed attached to the motive power depot in Queen Street, York. The smaller exhibits were found a home in a separate building, some few hundred yards away, and which had once been the first class refreshment rooms of the old York station.

It was in these locations that the LNER inherited the collection in 1923. Up to then, and indeed up to the Railway Centenary Celebrations in 1925, the collection slowly grew, but it was only possible to view the museum by special arrangement.

For the Centenary Celebrations a lot of the exhibits were placed on view at the

LNER wagon works at Faverdale, near Darlington. It was not until 1928, however, that the museum was open on a more or less full time basis during office hours.

In 1929 the Advertising Department had available a full set of lantern slides with lecture notes, which described many of the museum exhibits, these slides could be borrowed by schools and clubs. By 1931 an average of fifty persons a day were visiting the museum, and because of the increasing interest, a forty-six-page guide was published in 1933. The guide sold for 3*d* (1½p), but for schools parties, etc. an abridged version was available which cost 1*d* (½p).

Over the years many items were donated to the museum by the other main line companies, none of whom had any similar facilities of their own. The museum was closed throughout the Second World War, with most of the valuable items being evacuated to safer locations. It was not until 18 July 1947 that, at a small ceremony, Sir Ronald Mathews, the General Manager, declared the museum open once again.

The museum remained in the old buildings at York until the 1970s when the new National Railway Museum opened on property previously owned by the LNER and also at York.

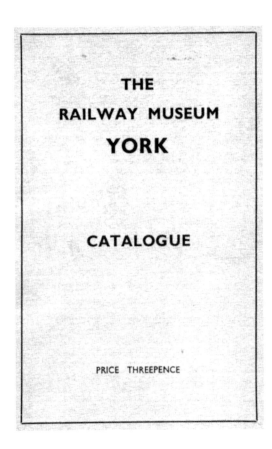

THE

RAILWAY MUSEUM

YORK

CATALOGUE

PRICE THREEPENCE

Two guide books were available to the LNER Railway Museum. This is the unabridged version dated 1933.

Carriage Panels

The first carriage panels were of course in use long before the formation of the LNER, but they were first used in carriages of the Great Eastern Railway, one of the LNER's constituent companies.

It was in fact the idea of William Worsdell, the Great Eastern's Locomotive Superintendent, who in 1884 felt that the company's carriages would be improved with the use of some photographic panels. His first thoughts were to provide some photographs of some of the company's hotels and larger stations and with this in mind he made contact with Payne Jennings, whose name at that time was very well known in the photographic world.

Following discussions with Payne Jennings it was realised that it would be a costly exercise for the rather hard up Great Eastern to provide photographs in all of their carriages, but it was suggested that if the photographic panels showed attractive views of some of the Great Eastern's holiday resorts, they would serve the dual purpose of advertisements as well as carriage decoration.

Worsdell thought the idea worth pursuing, and by 1886 2,000 Great Eastern carriages had Payne Jennings' panels installed. Although there was no conclusive proof that the carriage panels were responsible, it was noted that the number of passengers carried to the holiday resorts had risen since the panels had been provided.

The provision of carriage panels was soon taken up by the other railway companies, and by 1896 photographic carriage panels had become the norm. After the amalgamation the LNER continued with the use of photographs, but by now were also providing maps, mirrors and commercial advertisements.

For many years LNER carriages were provided with photographic panels such as this view of Cleethorpes.

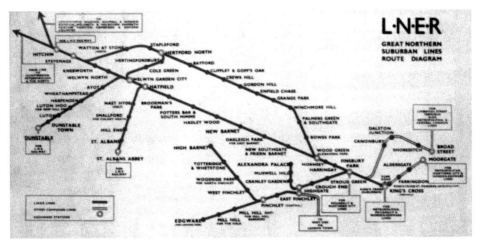

Shortly after joining the LNER, the late George Dow designed a number of carriage panel maps. This example is of the Great Northern and Great Eastern sections.

Prior to 1931 most of the LNER's commercial advertising was carried out by agents. This is a page from a small booklet published by Thomas McDougall who were the LNER's agents for the Great Northern and Great Eastern sections.

Tell the Stalls & Gallery too

"There were with me in the train this morning a Rural Dean, a grocer, two brokers, a married woman and a bricklayer. I imagine that no other form of advertising would interest them all so much as those clever, dignified pencil sketches that you see in L·N·E·R carriages nowadays. Anyhow, I noticed that all my fellow passengers saw and read them."

Your pencil advertisements in L·N·E·R carriages are seen by people of every class and circumstance who make 950,000 journeys every day. The quiet dignity of the pictures appeals to the eye. The mind has time to grasp your message. The low rates include provision of sketches and panels.

Say it in pencil to the Buyer Side of Britain

The late George Dow has related that shortly after joining the LNER's Press Section in 1929, he designed several carriage panel route maps for various parts of the system, and which were produced with the agreement of W.M. Teasdale.

The arrangements for commercial advertising panels was in the early days let out on an agency basis, with Thomas McDougall Ltd having the agency for the GE, GN and NE sections. It was in 1926 that McDougall's published a rather nice little booklet extolling the virtues of the LNER's carriage advertisements. The booklet showed examples of various artist-drawn advertisements for Lux Soaps, Swan Vesta Matches and several other well-known products, in an effort to attract more interest in this form of advertising.

From 1 April 1931 the LNER made the decision to deal with its own commercial carriage advertising, which was to include the design of the panel. This seemed to have almost immediate effect when a contract was signed with the manufacturers of Shredded Wheat to take 20,000 panels to advertise their breakfast cereals.

In common with the other railway companies, the LNER made great use of the carriage panel to advertise its own services such as freight and parcel deliveries and the shipping and hotel facilities.

It was Cecil Dandridge who in 1936 introduced a series of coloured scenic views to be used in the carriages of the new corridor stock then being constructed for the more important express services. The original series was of sixteen different views of some of the places on the system. The artists for these pictures were Frank Mason and C.H. Baraud.

This type of panel became more and more popular as replacements for the earlier photographic pictures, both on cost and in terms of visual presentation.

After 1931 the LNER took control of their own commercial advertising. Shown here is a carriage panel looking for business.

From 1936 the photographic carriage panel started to lose favour to watercolour prints which were cheaper to provide and more decorative. This is a later example showing High Wycombe.

Requests from the public to purchase the new prints were soon coming in, and the Advertising Department placed mounted versions on sale at the then not inconsiderable price of 10s 6d (52 ½p) each. In later years unmounted prints were sold in books of half dozen or so, but this fact never seems to have been advertised.

At the beginning of the Second World War most of the carriage panel maps were removed for security reasons, but these were shortly to be replaced with panels advising what to do in the event of an air raid and to be careful when travelling in the blackout. There were some standard panels of this type that were provided to all of the main line companies, but the LNER had its own rather nicer version with dark blue border and LNER elliptical totem.

After the war more use was made of the coloured print type of panel, which continued into nationalisation. This type of panel became standard on all regions of British Railways until, for various reasons, they were abolished in the 1970s.

Pictorial Luggage Labels

Railway luggage labels had been in use since the early days of the railway companies, and it is somewhat surprising that they were not used for publicity purposes to a greater degree.

The first LNER pictorial luggage labels were introduced around 1931, which was about the same time that the Great Western produced some pictorial labels for their 'Cheltenham Flyer' and 'Cornish Riviera' expresses.

The large rectangular LNER labels were designed by Frank Newbould, for which he was paid a fee of £15, and like the Great Western labels, the LNER versions were designed for some of the company's named trains such as the Flying Scotsman and the Queen of Scots, as well as some of the shipping services out of Harwich.

The idea of using pictorial luggage labels was first taken up by the LNER in 1931. Some large rectangular labels were designed by Frank Newbould, two of which are shown.

Unlike the Great Western's which did not seem to give any destination, the LNER's labels had the various destinations printed boldly on the label. Very little information is available on these early pictorials, and only a few seemed to have survived the passing years.

In 1936 a new set of large circular pictorial labels was introduced, again designed by Frank Newbould. Initially the labels were printed for the Flying Scotsman, the Silver Jubilee and the Yorkshire Pullman. Similar labels were also published for some of the company's shipping services out of Harwich, which included 'Week End Cruises'.

The Northern Belle cruise train was also catered for with both tie on and stick on labels. These had the date of the particular 'cruise', together with provision for the passengers name, address, and 'cabin' number on the bottom of the label. For 1938 these Northern Belle labels were additionally captioned 'The Coronation Year Cruise of the Northern Belle'.

Describing Newbould's excellent design, the *Railway Gazette* of the time said that 'both standard and streamlined locomotives were depicted on the labels'. In fact the label for the Flying Scotsman was of two designs, one showing the streamlined 2-8-2 locomotive of the P2 class, and the other showed a streamlined A4.

The design for the Queen of Scots and the Yorkshire Pullman labels depicted a Standard A3 Class locomotive, whilst those for the Silver Jubilee and the later to be added Coronation, of course showed a streamlined A4.

Identical pictorial labels were printed for the East Anglian, and these also depicted an A4 locomotive. However in the case of this particular train, this was technically incorrect. It will be recalled that the A4s were not used on this service, which made use of the two smaller but streamlined B17 locomotives. No doubt a little 'artistic licence' was allowed on occasions.

Newbould used a different combination of colours for the labels of each train and prominent among those was blue, black and silver for the Silver Jubilee and red, black and gold for the Flying Scotsman.

Upon the introduction of the West Riding service in 1937, similar labels were produced, but in this case it will be recalled that the Baynard Press had been commissioned with the whole design and print publicity package, and the labels therefore used 'Shep's' (J.C.M. Sheperd) stylised A4 design that was used on the posters and booklets.

With a British Railways heading, the circular pictorial luggage label design of the LNER was used well into nationalisation, and indeed with the introduction of some new named trains in the 1950s, was even extended.

In 1936 Newbould was asked to design a new range of pictorial luggage labels. These were the well-known circular labels some of which are shown here.

Chapter Eight

FOR SALE ITEMS

Postcards

In common with the other railway companies, the LNER published a considerable number of picture postcards. These 'official' postcards were produced for the company by various specialist manufacturers, amongst whom were The Photocrom Co., Valentine's, the Locomotive Publishing Co., Ben Johnson and Co., Messrs Hood of Middlesbrough, who also used the 'Sanbride' trademark, and W.H. Smith & Son who also produced cards under the 'Kingsway' and 'Bridge house' titles.

One would not have thought that the LNER could solve your Christmas present problems. An advertisement from the *Railway Magazine* of 1934.

L·N·E·R
SALE PUBLICATIONS

Attention is drawn to the undermentioned publications, issued by the London & North Eastern Railway, which may be obtained from any L·N·E·R Office or Bookstall, or by sending a remittance to the Passenger Manager, Liverpool Street Station, London, E.C.2

Holiday Handbook, 1938—Price 6d. each.

Completely revised guide for selecting a holiday centre on the " Drier Side," with tariffs of Hotels, Boarding Houses, etc., numerous illustrations in photogravure and maps

RAMBLE BOOKS—Price 6d. each

With maps and illustrations

London Area—
Rambles in Buckinghamshire
Rambles in the Chilterns
Rambles in Epping Forest
Rambles in Essex
Rambles in Hertfordshire
Rambles in Bucks.—Oxon.—Berks.

Provinces—
Rambles in Cambridgeshire
Rambles in Norfolk
Rambles in Suffolk
Rambles in Lincolnshire
Rambles in Nottinghamshire and The Dukeries
Walking and Cycling Tours in the Manchester District
Rambles in the Cleveland District of Yorkshire
Rambles on the Yorkshire Coast and Moors
Rambles in Durham and Northumberland

WALKS CARDS
Rambles around Edinburgh
Rambles around Glasgow
(Two colour maps with instructions on reverse)
12 Cards in special envelope ... ... 1s. 0d.
Single Cards ... ... 1d.

"DOMINION OF CANADA" TABLE LIGHTER

A Model in Colour of Streamlined Locomotive No. 4489

Fitted with chromium-plated petrol lighter and pull-out striker

10/6

A useful gift for home or office

Base measurement, $10\frac{1}{2}" \times 2\frac{1}{2}"$ Overall length of locomotive, 7"

"THE CORONATION"
Postcards
Front of Train showing Streamlined Engine
Rear of Train showing Beaver Tail Car
Two real photograph Postcards ... ... each   2d.

This handbill of 1938 shows some more 'for sale' items.

"WEST RIDING LIMITED"
Postcard
A real photograph of the Train (in preparation) ...

"THE SILVER JUBILEE"
Jig-saw Puzzle
Size 13 inches by 10 inches (175 pieces) ... ...
A real photograph postcard ... ...

"THE FLYING SCOTSMAN"
A Model of the Locomotive
Finished in oxidised silver, with a base measurement of inches by $1\frac{1}{2}$ inches. ...
Jig-saw Puzzle
Size $12\frac{1}{2}$ inches by 10 inches (175 pieces) ... ...

"SILVER LINK" LOCOMOTIVE No. 2509
A model of the Locomotive
Silver plated on oxidised silver base, $5\frac{3}{8}$ inches by $1\frac{1}{2}$ inch

STREAMLINED LOCOMOTIVES
Postcards
No. 2509   Silver Link
No. 4488   Union of South Africa
No. 4489   Dominion of Canada
No. 4490   Empire of India
No. 4491   Commonwealth of Australia
No. 4492   Dominion of New Zealand
No. 4496   Golden Shuttle
No. 4498   Sir Nigel Gresley
Real photograph postcards ... ... each   2d.

"THE CORONATION" AND OTHER FAMOUS L·N·E·R TRAINS
A 176-page book by Cecil J. Allen, M.Inst.T., with 92 pictures and 4 diagrams ... ... 1s. 0d.

"L·N·E·R LOCOMOTIVES"
With numerous illustrations and detailed information. Also contains list of L·N·E·R named engines ... ... 1s. 0d.

"A ROUND OF GOLF" by Bernard Darwin
Contains maps and complete list of courses on the L·N·E·R   1s. 0d.

"SALMON AND TROUT FISHING" by Jock Scott
Contains maps and complete list of fisheries on the L·N·E·R   1s. 0d.

Time Tables
Large: Containing all services except London Suburban ...   6d.
Small Pocket: London Suburban—G.C., G.E. and G.N. Sections ... ... 1d.
Liverpool and Manchester; Sheffield; Nottingham, Leicester and Rugby; West Riding; and Lincolnshire Districts   1d.
Eastern Counties ... ... 2d.
Pocket: N.E. Area ... ... 2d.   Scottish Area ...   3d.

Pictorial Posters published by L·N·E·R
Copies can be obtained from the Advertising Manager, 26, Pancras Road, King's Cross, N.W.1
Double-Royal size (25 in. by 40 in.) ... ... 2s. 6d.
Quad-Royal size (50 in. by 40 in.) ... ... 5s. 0d.

Very many LNER 'official' postcards were produced. This one shows RMS *Vienna*.

Perhaps rather strangely for a railway company, the greatest number of postcards featured the LNER's large fleet of ships, there being well over eighty different cards without counting various minor variations occurring with re-printing, etc.

The most pictured of the ships seems to have been the RMS *Prague*, this being closely followed by her sister ship the RMS *Vienna*, which together with the RMS *Amsterdam* were built in 1930 for the Harwich to Hook of Holland service.

Many thousands of postcards must have been written on board these ships as they crossed the North Sea, and particularly perhaps on board *Vienna* whilst on her summer weekend cruises, which was a speciality of this ship.

All of the company's ships were featured in at least one, if not more, postcards. Not to be left out were the Clyde Steamers. A new set of cards introduced in 1932 showed *Kenilworth*, *Marmion*, *Talisman*, *Jeanie Deans* and *Waverley*, these cards all selling for 1*d* (½p) each.

There does seem to be some doubt as to whether a postcard was ever published of the PS *Lincoln Castle*. Certainly cards are known of her sister ships on the Hull to New Holland ferry service, which were the paddle steamers *Wingfield Castle* and *Tattershall Castle* and there seems to be no good reason why *Lincoln Castle* should have been left out.

As a matter of interest it is thought that the longest surviving picture of any official railway postcard, was of the former Great Central Railway Co.'s ships *Dewsbury*, *Stockport* and *Accrington*. These appeared on a Great Central card of 1911 and which were used throughout the life of the LNER, and apparently were still being issued by the Associated Humber Lines Co. in 1967.

This 'official' LNER card was produced for the Railway Centenary of 1925. The back or address side was printed with the early LNER totem.

This 'official' of the LNER's North British Hotel, Edinburgh, was an earlier type that was overprinted in 1932 with a change of telephone number.

The second largest group of official postcards was of the company's twenty-three hotels and like the hotels themselves, several of the cards were inherited in the 1923 amalgamation.

There were well over sixty different postcards produced covering the hotels and again that is not counting for minor printing variations. The North British Hotel in Edinburgh appears to have been the subject of the largest group of hotel postcards.

In addition to several separate cards, a complete booklet of twelve tear-out cards was published in late 1930, showing views of, and from, the North British. These cards were on sale at the hotel for 1s (5p) per booklet, and are easily distinguished by their perforated left-hand edge.

During 1935 a series of double royal pictorial posters were produced showing interior scenes at some of the LNER hotels, and at least three of these were reproduced in postcard form for sale at the particular hotel.

Some of the earliest LNER cards were produced for the Railway Centenary celebrations in 1925. These included a black and cream card of *Locomotion No.1*. This card was by the Photocrom Co. and like most of the other cards was sold for 1d (½p). Another card by Photocrom was of 4472, *Flying Scotsman* and, like a similar card from the Locomotive Publishing Co., both were in full colour.

The Locomotive Publishing Co. also produced a set of twelve cards for the Centenary, among which were cards of the first railway timetable, the programme of the opening of the Stockton & Darlington Railway and a Stockton & Darlington timetable of 1837. This particular set of cards were half in sepia and half in colour and were sold for 1s 6d (7½p) the set. As well as being sold at the Centenary, these cards would almost certainly have been on sale on the LNER stand at the 1925 British Empire Exhibition.

It goes without saying of course, that several postcards were published showing the streamlined A4 locomotives, and these were produced for the company by the Locomotive Publishing Co. There were at least eight cards showing various A4s, together with cards of the streamline trains, such as the Coronation, West Riding Limited and Silver Jubilee. Although somewhat earlier, *Cock o' The North* was not left out, there were four cards of this lovely locomotive.

There were very high hopes for the so called 'hush-hush' *Locomotive 10000*, and in the early days of this engine a set of four postcards was produced for the LNER by Photocrom. These were sold in a special envelope for 8d (3p). This particular set of cards was first put on sale at the 1930 Schoolboys Exhibition, where it was said they sold like hot cakes.

At least four postcards were published for the 'cruise of the *Northern Belle*' and these sepia cards showed different views of the train 'on cruise', one of course at

Some 'officials' were sold in sets, like this example of Locomotive 10000.

There were several 'official' postcards showing the LNER's camping coaches. The scene shown here was of course posed.

the celebrated stopping place on Glenfinnan Viaduct, on the line from Fort William to Mallaig.

Hard on the heels of the launch of the first *Northern Belle* cruise train came the announcement of the LNER's Camping Coach arrangements, with the first lettings on 1 July 1933. It was not long before a series of official postcards of the Camping Coaches became available, and in fact in the early years of the scheme, it was arranged that a supply of ten free postcards were left in the coaches for the use of each new tenant. In later years the number of free cards was reduced, but as it was the local Stationmaster's job to service the coaches, no doubt further cards could be purchased from him if required.

CAMPING COACHES

are available at seaside and inland holiday districts throughout the L·N·E·R system in England and Scotland

THE ·CHARGE FOR A COACH TO ACCOMMODATE SIX PERSONS IS

£3 3 0

PER WEEK

Each Coach has two separate sleeping compartments (together accommodating six people) a living room and a kitchen, and is fully equipped

THERE IS ALSO A TOURING CAMPING COACH WHICH TRAVELS AROUND THE DALES AND MOORS OF YORKSHIRE

Ask for an illustrated folder giving full particulars at any L·N·E·R Station, Office or Agency

Any press advertisements were placed to advertise camping coaches. This one is of late 1930s vintage.

The Camping Coach postcards, of which seven types are known, were all sepia prints.

In 1934 the Locomotive Publishing Co. produced a set of twelve postcards for the LNER Railway Museum at York. These were, in the main, pictures of the various locomotives that were on exhibition, but one card was actually a photograph of the 'small exhibits' section of the museum.

The remaining known official LNER postcards are a dozen views of well-known places on the system, a card of the first wagon to be built at the company's Faverdal Works, Darlington, and three cards of the LNER's training centres at Watton House, Hertford, and Grantly House, Darlington.

The LNER Paperweight Models

It was during a meeting of the Passenger Managers' Committee at the beginning of 1928, that one of the Committee Members raised the point that the LMSR were producing ashtrays as an advertising medium. The Chairman asked Cecil Dandridge if he would care to comment on this matter, to which Dandridge replied that he would like to give the matter some thought and would report back to the committee in due course.

At a subsequent meeting of the committee held on 23 July, Dandridge reported that he had considered several possibilities as a counter to the LMS initiative, but he had finally made arrangements to have manufactured some metal paperweight models of the LNER's locomotive *Flying Scotsman*, which would be made available as a 'for sale' item of publicity.

SCALE MODEL

finished in

Oxidised Silver

of the famous

" FLYING SCOTSMAN " LOCOMOTIVE

which performed the

World's record daily non-stop run

KING'S CROSS–EDINBURGH

Post 2/6 free

From London & North Eastern Railway (Dept. R.M.), 26, Pancras Road, London, N.W.1; Passenger Manager, Liverpool Street Station, E.C.2; L·N·E·R, York; Waverley Station, Edinburgh; or Traffic Superintendent, L·N·E·R, Aberdeen; also at L·N·E·R Offices and Bookstalls.

LONDON &
NORTH EASTERN
RAILWAY

This advertisement of 1929 gives details of the first of the paperweight models.

A Silver Link paperweight model in later years.

The passing years have mellowed this Cock o' The North model.

The models were of cast metal with a rectangular base measuring just under 5in x 1½in and the finish was said to be oxidised silver. They were placed on sale for 2s 6d (12½p) and could be purchased from LNER Enquiry Offices, bookstalls or by post from the Passenger Managers office at Liverpool Street.

As a 'for sale' item, the *Flying Scotsman* paperweight proved very popular, and this led to the production of another model in June 1933. At this particular time *Locomotive 10000* was receiving a lot of publicity and it was decided to base the new paperweight on this engine. The new model was again priced at 2s 6d and was of identical size and finish as the original.

Once again the success of the two models encouraged Dandridge to produce two further examples, these were *Cock o' The North* in late 1934, and *Silver Link* in November 1935. Both these new models followed the original pattern, except that it was said that *Silver Link* had a 'silver-plated finish'.

The last of the paperweight models appeared in January 1938, and was a much grander example. It was advertised as a model in colour of streamlined locomotive 4489 *Dominion of Canada*. This model, which was made by Messers Mould Metals

"DOMINION OF CANADA"

TABLE LIGHTER

A Model in Colour of Streamline Locomotive No. 4489 of "The Coronation," fitted with chromium-plated petrol lighter and pull-out striker. Length of base 10½ ins. Overall length of locomotive 7 ins.

USEFUL FOR HOME OR OFFICE

10/6

(11/- post free)

Obtainable at L·N·E·R Offices and Bookstalls or from :

Advertising Department, L·N·E·R, 26, Pancras Road, London, N.W.1.

A 1938 advertisement for the last of the paperweight models, Dominion of Canada.

of London, had a base measurement of 10in x 2½in, and at one end of the model there was a chromium-plated cigarette lighter with a pullout striker. The model was finished in Garter Blue and was advertised as being 'a useful gift for home or office'. This last example was sold for 10*s* 6*d* (52½p) through the outlets as before.

Although the paperweight models were relatively expensive for the time, they were very popular with the public. A brief note in the *Magazine* in 1929 said that in the first year, no less than 1,224 models of *Flying Scotsman* had been mailed abroad. Unfortunately no sales figures ever seem to have been published for home sales.

The Cathedral Series Dessert Plates

During their years in office, both Teasdale and Dandridge had many novel ideas for advertising the LNER's services, a number of these were seriously looked at but financial constraints often precluded them being taken up. However Dandridge must have been somewhat pleased when, in October 1929, an idea he put before a meeting of the LNER's Hotel Managers was readily accepted. His suggestion was

ORDER FORM

L·N·E·R CATHEDRAL SERIES
DESSERT PLATES

To Hotels Superintendent, G.N. and G.C. Sections.
LONDON AND NORTH EASTERN RAILWAY,
366 Gray's Inn Road, London, W.C.1.

Please send to address given below
Dessert Plates (subjects as indicated), for which
I have { paid / enclose }   £   :   :

PLATES REQUIRED.	PLATES 2s. EACH.
Durham Cathedral.	
Ely Cathedral.	
Lincoln Cathedral.	PACKING AND POSTAGE
Norwich Cathedral.	1, 2 or 3 plates, 9d.
Peterborough Cathedral.	4, 5 or 6 plates, 1/-
York Minster.	

Name (Mr., Mrs., Miss)

Address

The LNER took a very innovative step when they introduced the series of Cathedral dessert plates as for sale items. To purchase the plates completion of the application form was required. Shown here are Ely Cathedral and York Minster.

to equip the company's restaurant cars (these were operated by the Hotels Department) with some special china dessert plates, that would not only be used by the diners, but would also be made available as a 'for sale' item.

The plates were to be made by the famous potteries of Josiah Wedgwood & Sons Ltd who were that very year celebrating the bi-centenary of the birth of their founder. The plates were described as being of the same shape and materials as plates made by Wedgwood's for the Empress Catherine of Russia in 1774.

Whilst the views and borders of the plates were in similar style to those on the original plates, the borders were actually formed of the rose and thistle that was incorporated in the LNER coat of arms. The views in the centre of the plates were of the six principle cathedrals located on the company's system, which were York Minster, Durham, Norwich, Peterborough, Lincoln and Ely.

The plates were originally provided on the restaurant cars on the East Coast, and Liverpool St-Harwich services. The plates could not, however, be purchased on the trains. The arrangement was that when dessert was being served, the diners would be handed a specially printed brochure that gave a potted history of Wedgwood's, and a description of the actual manufacturing process. At the back of the brochure was a short description of each of the cathedrals, and an order form which could be completed and handed to the attendant, or sent by post to the Hotels Superintendent.

The price of the plates was 2s (10p) each, and it was noted that over 750 had been sold in the first three months. It was after the first few months that the plates were also made available on the LNER's ships running out of Harwich.

It was reported that after some eighteen months from their introduction, over 2,600 plates had been sold, some having been sent to every country in Europe as well as to the USA and Canada.

A second and third series of the Cathedral Plates was issued by British Railways in the late 1940s and early 1950s. These appeared to differ from the originals with some colour changes and were printed on the reverse with the caption, 'Issued by courtesy of the London & North Eastern, Rly, England'.

It is thought that the LNER was the only railway company to sell souvenir china of this type.

LNER Playing Cards

Between the years 1925 and 1939, the firm of John Waddington & Co. of Leeds, produced around fifty different patterns of playing cards which were associated with the LNER. These playing cards were manufactured in Waddington's 'Beautiful Britain' series. The backs of the cards carried scenic views of places on the LNER system, and these were mainly in monochrome with several colour variations. There were however some early sets of cards in full colour.

Up to about 1930 the full London & North Eastern title appeared on each card together with the particular name of the place depicted, but after this date the company name was only printed on the 'ace of spades'.

Although at first glance this particular method of advertising would seem to be fairly ineffectual, it is believed that the only cost to the LNER was to supply Waddington's with the original pictures. In those days before television, whist was a very popular card game, and large numbers of these cards were used at 'whist drives'. In the *Magazine* for January 1931 it was noted that seventy-three packs of LNER playing cards had been used at a whist drive at Southampton.

In January 1931, Messrs Jaques & Son Ltd produced a card game under the title 'Counties of Britain'. The game was sold for 2s (10p) and came in a slip case bearing the title 'Counties of Britain Served by the London & North Eastern Railway'. There were forty-five cards in the game, thirty-six of which had small monochrome reproductions of well-known LNER pictorial posters of the period.

With the permission of the LNER, John Jaques & Co. published this card game in 1931. The cards all featured LNER posters of the time.

Beneath each picture there was a short descriptive text of the subject. These games were not 'official' LNER publicity material, but the manufacturers acknowledged the co-operation of the LNER for allowing reproduction of their posters.

Cardboard Cut-Outs, Diagrams and Pictures

What were some of the LNER's first for sale items were produced for the 'British Empire Exhibition' of 1924.

Among the books and postcards were cardboard cut-out models of *Flying Scotsman* and *Locomotion No.1*. The two models were on a single folded sheet of card, and were on sale at 6d (2½p) each. The sheet, which was in colour, was contained in a paper wrapper, which had full instructions on how to cut out and glue the parts together printed on the back. For the 1925 British Empire Exhibition similar cut out models of the latest type of sleeping carriage and the old 'Experiment' coach of 1825 were produced, again on a single folded sheet of card.

As before these were sold in a paper wrapper. These cardboard cut-out's were described as 'scale model sheets' and both items were also put on sale at the Railway Centenary Exhibition of 1925.

A somewhat unusual item was placed on sale during October 1933. This was first mentioned in the *Magazine* as being an 'interior plan' of *Locomotive 10000*. It was in fact a fine cutaway diagram of the locomotive with explanatory notes. The diagram had been commissioned from J.H. Clark of Plumstead, London, who specialised in 'cutaway' machinery and engineering drawings.

The 'interior chart', as it was to be advertised, was on sale to the public in a special envelope for 1s (5p) each, but could be purchased by members of staff for 6d (2½p).

The cardboard cut-out models were sold at the British Empire Exhibition in these paper wrappers.

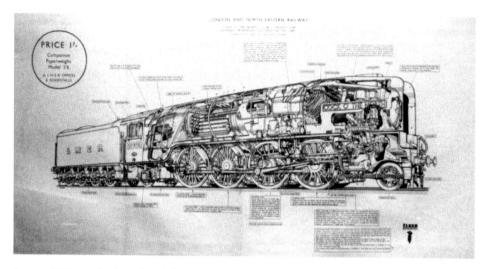

January 1935 saw the first sales of this 'interior diagram' of Cock o' The North. It was sold in the brightly coloured envelope shown.

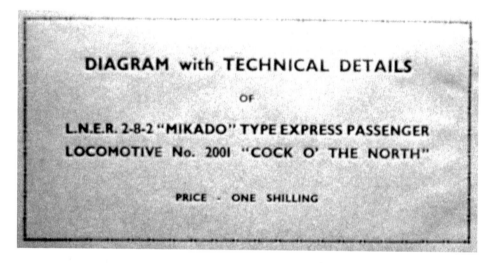

In January 1935 a similar 'interior chart' was published, this time showing *Cock o' The North*. As before, the superb drawing was by Harry Clark and again sold for 1*s*. These 'charts' were available up to the end of 1937, about which time they went out of print.

For several years coloured pictures of *Flying Scotsman* and *Locomotive 10000* were on sale. The pictures measured approximately 25in x 11in, and were sold for 1*s* 6*d* (7½p) and 1*s* (5p) each respectively.

This is the only jigsaw puzzle that was actually published by the LNER. It went on sale in 1931 and, of course, shows Locomotive 10000.

Jigsaw Puzzles

Unlike the Great Western Railway, who over the years published over forty different jigsaw puzzles, the LNER were only associated with three 'official' jigsaws.

It is not clear when the first LNER puzzle was produced, but it was certainly before 1930, and of course it featured the *Flying Scotsman*. The picture which measured 12½in x 10in showed the famous train with the usual A3 locomotive. The 175-piece puzzle was sold for 2*s* 6*d* (12½p), and it is only from the labelling on the box that one can ascertain its 'official' status.

Shown here is a small press advertisement for the LNER's puzzles.

JIG-SAW   PUZZLES
"THE SILVER JUBILEE"
and
"THE FLYING SCOTSMAN"
TRAINS
175 pieces **2/6** EACH

Obtainable at L·N·E·R Offices and Station Bookstalls.

This Victory jigsaw puzzle, although not 'official', was published with permission of the LNER.

The next jigsaw was introduced toward the end of 1931 and pictured *Locomotive 10000*. This time the picture was a little larger at 25in x 11in, and was made up of 160 pieces which sold for 5*s* (25p) each.

The puzzle of *10000* was produced for the LNER by the Photocrom Co. and was a rather stark view of the 'hush hush' locomotive against a plain yellow background. In this instance it clearly stated on the lower margin that the puzzle was published by The London & North Eastern Railway.

The last LNER jigsaw was produced at the end of 1935. The 13in x 10in picture was of the *Silver Jubilee* being taken out of Kings Cross by the locomotive *Silver Link*. The 175-piece puzzle was sold for 2*s* 6*d* (12½p) and was produced by Hayters under their 'Victory' trade name.

This was the last of the 'official' LNER jigsaw puzzles. it was manufactured by Hayters under their 'Victory' label but was sold by the LNER as a sale item.

Helensburgh as seen by Frank Mason in 1941. The publication of this double royal was held over until 1946 because of the Second World War.

York Minster is shown in this double royal. Fred Taylor actually completed it in 1941 but because of the Second World War it was also not published until 1946.

This 1947 picture of Norfolk by John Bee was among a small series he did for the LNER just prior to nationalisation.

Appendix 1

THE LNER TOTEMS/LOGOS

The Totems or Logos used by the LNER are shown with approximate periods used. The dates however are for general guidance only and should not be taken as precise. For instance a Type 1 Totem has been seen on a publication dated 1928.

TYPE 1. Designed just prior to amalgamation in 1923 and used in 1923 and mid-1924.

TYPE 2. Used from mid-1924 to1928. Used extensively during this period on posters, handbills, booklets, etc.

TYPE 3. 1928-1932. This design was almost certainly by Tom Purvis and was used on posters, etc. It was also used on some modernised stations of the period.

TYPE 4. 1933-1934. This was the original design by Eric Gill.

TYPE 5. 1934 until nationalisation on 1 January 1948. Eric Gill's totem was altered to this arguably more pleasing design which was used on all types of advertising, as well as stations, road vehicles, uniforms etc.

A great deal of advertising material was produced using just the company's initials, two styles of which are shown. Style 'A' was in use in 1923 and appeared with and without an enclosing rectangle. Style 'B' is of later 1930s vintage and uses Gill Sans typeface.

STYLE 'A'

STYLE 'B'

L·N·E·R

It is perhaps worth noting that the original British Railways totem was designed in the first few weeks of nationalisation, by the LNER's last Advertising Manager, A.J. White.

Appendix 2

LIST OF REGISTERED NUMBER PUBLICATIONS FOR THE YEAR 1935

1) *The Holiday Handbook.* Price 6d
2) *Holiday Guide to Eastern Counties*
3) *Holiday Guide to North East England*
4) *Scotland for the Holidays* (Issued jointly with LMS)
5) *New Ways for British Holidays* (East Anglia)
6) *New Ways for British Holidays* (Lincolnshire and the Dukeries)
7) *New Ways for British Holidays* (Yorkshire Dales)
8) *New Ways for British Holidays* (Yorkshire Coast)
9) *New Ways for British Holidays* (Northumberland and Durham)
10) *On Either Side* (East Anglia)
11) *On Either Side* (East Coast Route)
12) *Guide to London* (Issued jointly with LMS)
13) *Through the Trossachs* (Issued jointly with LMS)
14) *Clyde and Loch Lomond* (Issued jointly with LMS)
15) *Land Of Scott and Burns* (Issued jointly with LMS)
16) *Publication Cancelled*
17) *Camping Holidays*
18) *Summary of Passenger Train Facilities*
19) *Cheap Party Travel* (Southern Area)
20) *Cheap Party Travel* (North Eastern Area)
21) *Cheap Party Travel* (Scotland)
22) *Inclusive Holidays*
23) *Large Party Outings Guaranteed Excursion Booklet* (North Eastern Area)
24) *Weekly Holiday Season Tickets* (Southern and North Eastern Area)
25) *Weekly Holiday Season Tickets* (Scottish Areas)
26) *Tourist Ticket Fares From London*
27) *Tourist Ticket Fares* (North East Area – Northern District)
28) *Tourist Ticket Fares* (North East Area – Central District)
29) *Tourist Ticket Fares* (North East Area – Southern District)
30) *Tourist Ticket Fares* (Scotland)
31) *Circular Tours in England and Scotland by Rail, Road and Steamer*
32) *Programme of Tours in Scotland by Rail, Road and Steamer* (Joint with LMS)

Abroad

33) *Holland via Harwich*
34) *Belgium and Luxembourg via Harwich*
35) *Germany via Harwich*
36) *Walcheren (Holland) via Harwich*
37) *Wandering on the Continent* (Youth Hostels)
38) *Belgian Coast via Harwich-Zeebrugge Summer Service Folder* (London Edition)
39) *Belgian Coast via Harwich-Zeebrugge Summer Service Folder* (Provincial Edition)
40) No Publication Listed
41) *Cheap Holiday Tickets to Holland, Belgium and Germany via Harwich, Grimsby or Hull*
42) *Holland via Harwich Time Table Folder*
43) *Germany via Harwich Time Table Folder*
44) *Belgium via Harwich Time Table Folder*
45) *Switzerland via Harwich Time Table Folder*
46) *Five Routes to and from the Continent via Harwich. Time Table Folder*
47) *Continent via Dublin-Liverpool, etc. Time Table Folder*
48) *Motor Car Rates to the Continent via Harwich, Folder*
49) *Week End Cruises from Harwich, Pictorial Folder*
50) *Northern Germany and Belgium via Grimsby*
51) *Hull-Rotterdam Pictorial Folder*

Appendix 3

CHECKLIST OF LNER PLAYING CARDS

1925	Norwich, Scarborough
1926	Norwich, Scarborough (two styles), Clacton-on-Sea, Edinburgh, Fort William, Nort Berwick, Royal Deeside, The Norfolk Broads, The Yorkshire Coast, York, Caister Castle, Cromer, Forth Bridge, The Trossachs, Whitby.
1927	Bamburgh Castle, Fountains Abbey, Lowestoft, Scarborough.
1928	Bamburgh Castle, Fountains Abbey, Lowestoft, Scarborough, Bridlington, Calton Hill, Cruden Bay, Felixstowe, Harrogate, Houses of Parliament, Hungerford Bridge, Newcastle-on-Tyne, Richmond, Royal Deeside, Whitby, York.
1930-1935	Cambridge, Ely Cathedral, Fountains Abbey, Loch Long, Melrose Abbey, Norwich, On The Yorkshire Coast, The Forth Bridge, The Norfolk Broads, Tower and Tower Bridge, Westminster Abbey & Houses of Parliament, York Minster.
1938-1939	Buckingham Palace, Norwich Cathedral, Royal Deeside, The Forth Bridge, The Norfolk Broads, Tower and Tower Bridge.

Appendix 4

THE LNER ADVERTISING DEPARTMENT'S EXPENDITURE ACCOUNTS FOR THE YEARS 1929-1938

1929 – £322,031	1934 – £225,315
1930 – £294,188	1935 – £234,204
1931 – £229,785	1936 – £237,193
1932 – £236,751	1937 – £246,623
1933 – £213,179	1938 – £259,693

CHECKLIST OF THE ORIGINAL SERIES OF SIXTEEN WATERCOLOUR CARRIAGE PANEL PRINTS INTRODUCED IN 1936

Print size 16in x 6in. With mounting, overall size 20in x 10in. Sold mounted for 10s 6d (52½p) each.

By Frank H. Mason
  Lowestoft, Fountains Abbey, Scarborough, Durham, Western Highlands, Bruges, The Rhine, Night Parade From Harwich.

By Cyril H. Barraud
  Cambridge, Felixstowe, Edinburgh, Royal Deeside, Holland, Lincoln, York, Knaresborough.

CHECKLIST OF CARRIAGE PANEL ROUTE MAPS DESIGNED BY THE LATE GEORGE DOW, WHO WAS WITH THE LNER'S PRESS SECTION

Most of the maps are in black, red and white.

Great Eastern London Suburban Lines	1929
Great Northern London Suburban Lines	1929
MSJ&A Electric Lines	1930
Great Central London Suburban Lines	1932
Tyneside Electric Lines (Including South Shields Line)	1938
Tyneside Electric Lines (Excluding South Shields Line)	1940
South Shields Line	1940

Appendix 6

THE GILL SANS TYPEFACE

The Gill Sans typeface, designed by Eric Gill for the Monotype Corporation in 1929, was adopted by the LNER and became a central feature of its printing and signing policy. The typeface is in popular use today in upper and lower case and in a great range of sizes and weights.

In order to help the reader more readily identify Gill Sans from other typefaces, a sample of uppercase lettering is appended below. The underlined letters should be particularly noted for ease of identification. It will be noticed that all chapter headings in this book are set in Gill Sans.

MONOTYPE GILL SANS

THE QUICK BR<u>OW</u>N FOX JUMPS OVER THE LAZY DO<u>G</u>

L N E <u>R</u>

<u>W</u> <u>G</u>